# *The* ADHD
# Empowerment
# Guide

# *The* ADHD
# Empowerment
## Guide

*Identifying Your Child's Strengths and Unlocking Potential*

James W. Forgan, Ph.D., & Mary Anne Richey

PRUFROCK PRESS INC.
WACO, TEXAS

Library of Congress Cataloging-in-Publication Data

Names: Forgan, James W., author. | Richey, Mary Anne, 1947- author.
Title: The ADHD empowerment guide : identifying your child's strengths and
   unlocking potential / James W. Forgan, Ph.D., and Mary Anne Richey.
Description: Waco, TX : Prufrock Press Inc., [2019] | Includes
   bibliographical references.
Identifiers: LCCN 2019001592 (print) | LCCN 2019002671 (ebook) | ISBN
   9781618218728 (eBook) | ISBN 9781618218711 (pbk.)
Subjects: LCSH: Attention-deficit hyperactivity disorder--Treatment. |
   Attention-deficit-disordered children--Treatment. | Parent and child.
Classification: LCC RJ506.H9 (ebook) | LCC RJ506.H9 F665 2019 (print) | DDC
   618.92/8589--dc23
LC record available at https://lccn.loc.gov/2019001592

Edited by Katy McDowall

Cover and layout design by Allegra Denbo
Illustrations by Micah Benson

ISBN-13: 978-1-61821-871-1

Printed in the United States of America.

At the time of this book's publication, all facts and figures cited are the most current available. All telephone numbers, addresses, and website URLs are accurate and active. All publications, organizations, websites, and other resources exist as described in the book, and all have been verified. The authors and Prufrock Press Inc. make no warranty or guarantee concerning the information and materials given out by organizations or content found at websites, and we are not responsible for any changes that occur after this book's publication. If you find an error, please contact Prufrock Press Inc.

Prufrock Press Inc.
P.O. Box 8813
Waco, TX 76714-8813
Phone: (800) 998-2208
Fax: (800) 240-0333
http://www.prufrock.com

# Dedication

Jim dedicates this book to his supportive family and Drs. Mangrum, Strichart, and Forgan, who were instrumental in unlocking his potential.

Mary Anne dedicates this book to Matthew, Maxwell, Molly, Cole, and Teddy, with thanks for all of the joy and wonder they have brought.

# Table of Contents

# Acknowledgements

Projects like this require the work of many individuals, and we'd like to thank Katy McDowall, our editor at Prufrock Press, for her expertise; Danielle Pettifor and Emily Forgan for their research; Rachel Salinger for her strategies; Drs. Michelle Chaney and Judith Aronson-Ramos for their contributions; and our loving spouses for their support.

# Introduction

This book is different than the previous books we've written to help parents of children with Attention Deficit/Hyperactivity Disorder (ADHD) and executive functioning difficulty. Inside these pages we have explained how we have parented our own children and helped other parents in our private practices unlock the potential in their children with ADHD. We want you and significant others to look at your child and not just see him as he is today, but instead forecast the future of what he can become. You have an amazing child who happens to have ADHD. As one of our teen clients used to say, "ADHD won't stop me," and we have faith that it won't stop your child either.

Just by reading this book you've demonstrated that you believe in your child. That is one of the secrets for unlocking your child's potential. We'll admit that children with ADHD can be annoying and get on your last nerve. But you still love your child. You still want the best for her. In order for your child to work toward her potential, she must have an adult who can sense the greatness and hidden treasure within. As all kids grow and develop, they are works in progress, but children with ADHD need even more guidance and support than their peers without ADHD. If your child has ADHD, she is less emotionally mature than peers and has more challenges to overcome with regard to inattentiveness, disorganization, impulsiveness, and emotional inconsistency. This just means your child needs you more than ever, so we want to encourage and equip you to help her.

From our experiences, we believe your child's potential is there. You may even be privy to small glimpses of that potential when he smiles because he has made you laugh, when he has independently finished homework, when he has made a right choice, or when he has told you about helping a friend. These glimpses are narrow windows that allow you to see a wonderful future for your child. It's easy to say everything will be all right, but when you sense that your child has what it takes to be successful, it's exciting. The passage of time will reveal the reward of your investments and perseverance in helping your child. We're pleased to accompany you on that journey. Here is how we have structured the book.

First, we'll give you some background information about ADHD, discuss characteristics that have enabled people with ADHD and learning disabilities to succeed, and highlight lives of successful people with ADHD along with advice they offer. Then, we'll introduce and explain the multiple intelligences theory. We believe a multiple intelligences approach to describing children with ADHD is the best way to capture their gifts and affinities. Children with ADHD can be smart in many ways, but standardized tests do not always fully capture their intelligence. Our children are outside-of-the-box thinkers, movers, and learners, who have gifts that emerge in myriad ways.

It's fine to be intelligent, but that alone does not equal success. There are many personal characteristics that are equally—if not more—important for success. We'll introduce 11 keys that are crucial for success in almost any field and for happiness in general. You'll learn about activities to improve any weaker areas and enhance your child's multiple intelligences.

If your child is 8 or older, we encourage you to give her an age-appropriate explanation of how you'll be helping to set her up for a successful future. We wrote two letters for children to read and feel encouraged. You can read them, and you may want to share one with your child.

# Introduction

Treating ADHD is an important part of unlocking your child's potential. We have included a chapter on current traditional and supplemental treatments, including articles by a developmental pediatrician and a child and adolescent psychiatrist. There are also four important questions to consider before medicating your child. We also encourage coaching for children with ADHD and offer insights and resources.

Because your child spends the majority of his day in school, it's important to have the right school fit. As school psychologists, we spent a lot of time working in schools, so we have a chapter dedicated to providing insight into school issues. In order to help you obtain the best school services for your child if he needs them, you'll find two sample letters that you can utilize to request a 504 plan or an Individualized Education Plan (IEP).

We recommend that you don't skip the final chapter because we will guide you through writing a brief plan for your child's future.

In summary, the steps for unlocking your child's potential include:

1. identifying your child's natural intelligences,
2. nurturing these areas through enrichment activities and experiences,
3. identifying your child's personal and extrinsic keys to success that need to be strengthened,
4. improving your child's weaker keys to success,
5. identifying and using the best treatments for ADHD,
6. seeking and receiving support from others, and
7. celebrating each small accomplishment.

As you read, you'll notice that we alternate between the pronouns "he" and "she." Regardless of the pronoun used, we are referring to your child, so simply substitute your child's name for the pronoun.

Helping your child is hard work, and one day she will realize this. Thank you for making a difference, and our compassion goes out to you.

# Chapter 1

# Success With ADHD

When you catch a glimpse of your potential, that's when passion is born.

—Zig Ziglar

## Laying the Foundation for Success With ADHD

Perhaps you have never really considered your child's potential, and that is okay. The purpose of this book is to give you additional tools to help determine your child's greatest assets and any shortcomings that might make it difficult to develop those strengths to the fullest.

We'd like you to begin by considering the question, "Is what I am currently doing to help unlock my child's potential working?" We know you are already busy and supporting a child with ADHD adds another layer to your hectic day. However, as parents and school psychologists dealing with ADHD, we know that the effort you put forth in learning the latest research and techniques for supporting your child will pay big dividends. We want to help guide you to *enjoy* rather than *endure* raising a child with ADHD.

Every family's journey of raising a child with ADHD is different. Yet, there is a common thread that we all share—a disorder that is hidden because it is brain-based but one that manifests in very real ways. Our children have a condition that is proven through neurological studies, including MRIs and other brain scans. Some teachers, relatives, and others want to chalk it up to simply bad behavior or poor parenting, but nothing is further from the truth. By increasing your understanding of ADHD and how to effectively work with your child, you can be more proactive in helping others be supportive as well.

# Behaviors Associated With ADHD

The core symptoms of ADHD are developmentally inappropriate levels of inattention, hyperactivity, and/or impulsivity. We all know the children who blurt out things before thinking about their consequences, can't sit or stay still, are accident prone, and are constantly in trouble with their teachers. However, these same children can hyperfocus and spend hours doing things that are stimulating or interesting to them. The children who are daydreamers are harder to spot than the hyperactive ones, but they have just as real a disability.

*We want you to know that you will likely be the number one influence on your child's future.*

We now know that children with ADHD also have deficits in executive functioning—the brain-based skills required to get tasks done. These skills include things like planning, starting, organizing, persevering, and completing tasks. Such skills are developmental in nature and can be improved with coaching and teaching. To make executive functioning easier to understand, some have compared it to the CEO or conductor of the brain. To fully understand ADHD in your child, it is important to know something about his level of executive functioning. If your child has trouble getting started on homework, he may not be oppositional or lazy; he may have deficient executive functioning in the area of initiation. We talk much more about these important skills in Chapter 4.

ADHD occurs on a continuum from very mild to very severe. Your child's severity affects your journey. Regardless of where your child is on this continuum, she has unlimited potential and can be successful if given the right support along the way.

We want you to know that you will likely be the number one influence on your child's future. The things you say to your child fill her head. The guidance, or lack of, shapes her decisions. The lessons you teach create a foundation. Success does not happen on its own. If you want your child to reach her potential, become intentional about your actions. Your child is a unique individual with a purpose in life. Part of your job as a parent is to provide your child with words of encouragement, guidance, and experiences to help her discover a purpose. Better than anyone, you know your child's natural strengths and weaknesses.

# Views of Success

## *Our Thoughts on Success*

Your definition of success depends on your culture, background, and values. There is no universal definition of success because people are unique in how they view the world. Some see success as having wealth, being a celebrity, or achieving important status in a career. Even Merriam Webster's definition of success includes having a "favorable or desired outcome; the attainment of wealth, favor." However, we read almost every day about someone who might be considered "successful" according to those standards but is miserable and unproductive. We define success as being happy with yourself and with what you have and believing that you make a difference in this world. When we talk with parents about what success would look like for their child, we hear things like the following: an independent person who supports himself as an adult, a quality person who can be counted on, and an effective problem solver who is able to use her talents to the betterment of herself and others.

*We define success as being happy with yourself and with what you have and believing that you make a difference in this world.*

Are you successful? Most people would answer this question with, "Yes, I'm successful in (insert a particular area in your life)." If you are like us, you are more successful in some areas as compared to others. Now relate this to your child. With all of the academic pressure on your child, just remember that academics is just one area. Your child's success in life does not mean earning stellar grades. Jim works with tweens and teens who struggle with learning and often feel discouraged or inadequate about their grades. He will ask them, "Do you think I'm successful?" When they answer, "Yes," he shows them his fourth-grade report card that had a lot of C grades (see Figure 1). They quickly understand that even a C student can be successful with support and hard work.

## What Some of the Experts Say About Success

In their 2018 book, *The Yes Brain Child*, Drs. Daniel Siegel and Tina Payne Bryson defined what they call "Yes Brain" success. They said success is "based on helping our children stay true to who they are while guiding them as they build skills and abilities that allow them to interact with the world from a place of balance, resiliency, insight, and empathy" (p. 164). Siegel and Bryson termed this "authentic success" because children are open to learning from new experiences and can handle any resulting adversity with a fuller understanding of themselves, their strengths, and their passions. This thinking fits with our definition of success and the focus of this book—helping our chil-

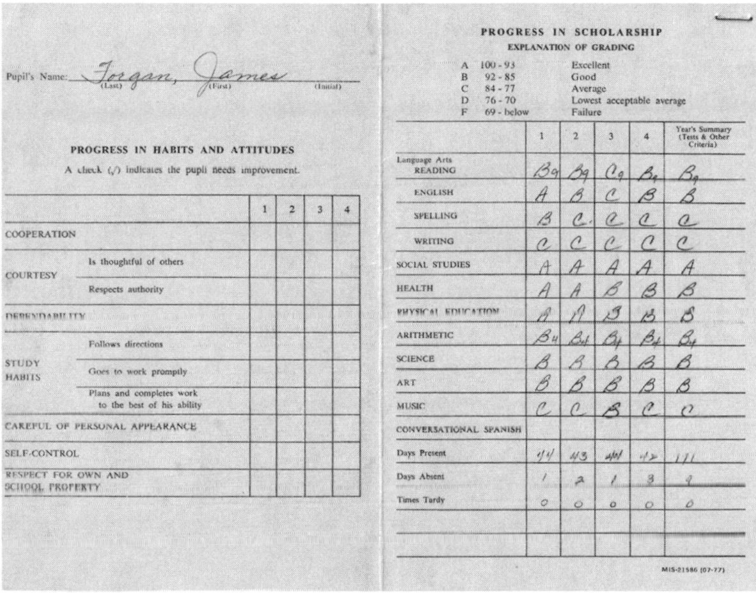

*Figure 1.* Jim's fourth-grade report card.

dren develop their skills to the best of their abilities, see challenges as opportunities, remain resilient in the face of setbacks, and be able to show concern and awareness for the needs of others.

Drs. Theresa Maitland and Patricia Quinn, authors of *Ready for Take-Off: Preparing Your Teen With ADHD or LD for College* (2011), studied what helps children with ADHD become successful adults. They believed success involves having a sense of self-determination, which requires an awareness of strengths and weaknesses and being able to set goals and work toward achieving them, including finding and using help when necessary. According to Maitland and Quinn, "Most importantly, a self-determined individual can solve problems, make decisions, and regulate his own behavior. Success in college and in life requires self-determination skills so young adults can take the controls effectively and overcome any obstacles that stand in the way" (p. 95).

Catharine Corman, a mother of triplets with ADHD, and Dr. Edward Hallowell, a psychiatrist, author, and speaker, who was diagnosed with ADHD at age 31, profiled successful people with ADHD in their book *Positively ADD: Real Success Stories to Inspire Your Dreams* (2006). Corman and Hallowell highlighted people who are proud of their accomplishments and their situation in life even though they did not often have an easy road. According to the authors, "While people with ADHD can achieve great success and find true happiness, they rarely do so by conventional routes. They often need more time than those without ADHD to figure things out and to thrive. False starts and true blunders are par for the course" (p. xviii). Corman and Hallowell recommended viewing ADHD as a strength—a "gift" that can be "unwrapped."

## What Society Says About Success for People With ADHD

Have you ever wondered if individuals with ADHD use their talents in ways that others don't? You may have read articles in which ADHD is considered to be a gift that enables people to become successful entrepreneurs and CEOs. Being able to hyperfocus, multitask, see solutions that others don't, and have a creative flair can definitely be an asset if the skills are managed properly. Through reading the histories of many of these people with ADHD, you find that they have often had their share of failures. What often sets them apart is their ability to make the most of their talents because of other characteristics, such as perseverance and resilience. Whether you child is destined to become an entrepreneur, an effective teacher, a helpful sales associate, or a competent electrician, helping him understand his strengths and assisting him in developing personal characteristics that lead to success will be invaluable to both of you.

# Success With ADHD

## *Your Concept of Success*

Success with ADHD has a lot to do with how you look at it. Success is a perspective. If you focus on the negative, you will reinforce negative traits in your child; if you focus on strengths, you build more positive traits in your child.

You may think worrisome thoughts about your child, but when you say them aloud, you give life to those words. When children hear their parents say negative things, they may internalize those thoughts and then act on them because they believe what mom or dad says. If you constantly tell your child, "You are bad," your child may believe, "I'm bad, so I'll act that way." If you say your child is lazy and unmotivated, you may create a self-fulfilling prophecy.

For example, Sally's mother was very fearful that Sally would not pass her annual state-mandated testing. She said to Sally, "I'm concerned that you will not pass the state testing, and then you will be held back." From this statement, Sally's own fears may be confirmed, and she may start to think, "I probably won't pass the test." Over time, this could lower her belief in her test-taking ability. Her mother could have acknowledged that the test would be difficult but encouraged Sally to do her best by preparing for it and seeing it as opportunity to show what she has learned rather than something to be feared.

> *If you want your child with ADHD to be successful, you must be intentional.*

We don't want to alarm you, but we are realists. Many children with ADHD seem to have the deck stacked against them if they are not fortunate enough to have the right treatment, support, and guidance. ADHD does not have to keep your child from being successful. When you learn your child has ADHD, how you approach it is part of what makes the difference between sorrow and success. You can view it from a problem perspective (i.e., "life's going to be tough") or a positive perspective (i.e., "we'll make the best of it").

If you want your child with ADHD to be successful, you must be intentional. This means that reaching success will take *a lot* of work. Some of our clients tell us they spend so much time learning about ADHD and how to help their child with ADHD that it feels like a second job. What does success mean for your child? Based on what you know and have read, write down your definition of success. If your child is old enough, include her in this exercise.

## CONSIDER THIS

What is your definition of success?

_____

_____

_____

# Helping Your Child Achieve Optimal Success

*An Overview of Our Process*

To help you recognize and nurture your child's natural abilities while improving some of the characteristics that could keep her from using her gifts, we developed two surveys: a Multiple Intelligences Profile and a Keys to Success Survey (described further in Chapters 3 and 4; see also Appendix). We created these tools based on our research involving multiple intelligences, as well as factors that contribute to success in children with ADHD and learning disabilities. We reviewed research and studies by Howard Gardner (1983, 1995) and others who studied multiple intelligences, along with success attribute researchers at the Frostig Center (Goldberg, Higgins, Raskind, & Herman, 2003) and others who have studied children with learning disabilities and ADHD.

Our surveys combine research and our experience as parents and professionals. Our belief is that to unlock your child's potential you must identify his top multiple intelligences and develop them. Then, you must identify any weaknesses in the Keys to Success Survey and work to strengthen them. We've seen this work with our own children and our clients' children. Table 1 is a brief summary of the two tools. In Chapter 3, you will learn more about your child's Multiple Intelligences Profile, and Chapter 4 describes the Keys to Success and how to strengthen any weaknesses.

## More on Multiple Intelligences

For most people, success does not occur without intention. If you interview any successful person, he or she won't say, "Well, you know, I just woke up one day and found myself at the top. I don't know how it happened, but I'll take it." Successful people will tell you that becoming successful takes hard work, persistence, and daily action. Some successful people are innovative thinkers who see faster, better, or more efficient ways to get things done or solve problems. Many of our kids with ADHD have innovative mindsets, move to the beat of their own drums, and learn in unconventional ways. They have a natural ability to see the world through a different lens than folks without ADHD. Our kids have multiple intelligences that shine in more ways than one. At times, their potential can even be hidden and just waiting to be discovered.

In his 1983 book, *Frames of Mind: The Theory of Multiple Intelligences*, Dr. Howard Gardner discussed his theory of multiple intelligences, which includes visual-spatial, bodily-kinesthetic, linguistic, interpersonal, logical, musical, and intrapersonal intelligence.

*Table 1*
Brief Summary of the Success Surveys

| Multiple Intelligences Profile | Keys to Success Survey |
|---|---|
| • Visual-Spatial Intelligence<br>• Bodily-Kinesthetic Intelligence<br>• Linguistic Intelligence<br>• Interpersonal Intelligence<br>• Logical Intelligence<br>• Musical Intelligence<br>• Intrapersonal Intelligence<br>• Naturalistic Intelligence | • Motivation<br>• Emotional Stability and Behavioral Control<br>• Integrity<br>• Social Skills<br>• Grit<br>• Organization<br>• Resilience<br>• Resourcefulness<br>• Appropriate School Setting<br>• Support Systems<br>• Use of Technology |

He later added a naturalistic category (Gardner, 1995). The multiple intelligences theory defines intelligence as a broad construct, and a child can be smarter in certain areas than others. The theory was created to help explain how the mind works. For instance, some children are highly intelligent in using technology, fixing things, building, drawing, or competing in athletics. They may just be average in academics or even struggle to read or do math. Traditional IQ testing does not use a multiple intelligence approach.

Children with ADHD are insightful and bring cleverness into their daily dealings with others. They often have strengths in two or more of these areas of intelligence—strengths that may offer the highest potential for their future career or success. Moran, Kornhaber, and Gardner (2009) wrote, "Adopting a multiple intelligences approach can bring about a quiet revolution in the way students see themselves and others. Instead of defining themselves as either 'smart' or 'dumb,' students can perceive themselves as potentially smart in a number of ways" (p. 188).

Thomas Armstrong writes books for classroom teachers on how to use the multiple intelligences framework within schools. He described his initial attraction to the theory because it "provided a language for talking about inner gifts of children, especially those students who have been given labels such as 'LD' and 'ADHD' during their school careers" (Armstrong, 2009, p. 1). The multiple intelligence theory helps us move away from mainly seeing the deficits caused by ADHD, to seeing a tool to identify strengths in children. Others have embraced this ideology and created teaching activities and frameworks for children with and without ADHD.

Proulx-Schirduan, Shearer, and Case (2009) wrote *Mindful Education for ADHD Students: Differentiating Curriculum and Instruction Using Multiple Intelligences* to provide instructional ideas and curriculum. They wrote that, when children with ADHD are looked at through the lens of a multiple intelligences curriculum, "ADHD is not a disadvantage; it is rather an integral component of how the student processes information, makes sense of the world, self-regulates, and ultimately acts" (p. xi). Imagine how children with ADHD would be taught and parented if more people used the multiple intelligence lens. We could embrace these children's energy, enthusiasm, struggles, and strife, while recognizing their potential to grow up and become tomorrow's trailblazers in their families and careers.

## More on Keys to Success

Throughout the past three decades, different groups have studied success factors in children with learning disabilities. Researchers' identification of success attributes in individuals with learning disabilities is relevant because an estimated 76% of individuals with ADHD also have learning disabilities (Mayes & Calhoun, 2007). Some movements in research often consider students with ADHD and students with learning disabilities as an integrated group, having similar needs for academic supports (Prevatt & Young, 2014). The Frostig Center researchers (Raskind, Goldberg, Higgins, & Herman, 1999; Spekman, Goldberg, & Herman, 1992, 1993) studied students with learning disabilities (LD) to determine which factors helped them have successful adult outcomes. They identified factors that include self-awareness, proactivity, goal setting, perseverance, support systems, and coping strategies.

As part of her longitudinal research, Werner (1993) studied individuals with learning disabilities in Kauai, HI, to determine factors of resiliency. She found protective factors that contributed to the individuals' success included:

- being satisfied as employed or in school,
- being married or in a long-term relationship,
- having positive relationship with their children,
- having close friends, and
- being mostly satisfied with their present state of life.

The research helped identify qualities that foster successful adaptation despite the associated risks and challenges of having LD or ADHD. Similarly, Gerber and Ginsberg (1990) studied employed adults with LD and found their success stemmed from setting goals for themselves. These individuals recognized their disability, accepted it, understood it, and took action. They selected jobs that were good fits for their interests, persisted, adapted, and surrounded themselves with supportive people.

Limited research exists on success attributes in individuals with ADHD. Sibley and Yeguez (2018) studied young adults with ADHD and reported success attributes, including having age-appropriate privileges and responsibilities, learning how to manage one's ADHD treatment, creating structure and routines, and using technology. Sulla (2017) studied college students to determine which factors supported success in students with ADHD. Based on her research with 10 individuals, she reported her participants' success in college was due to six factors:

- their interest in an academic subject and love of learning,
- awareness of learning style,
- internal drive and perseverance,
- technology,
- engagement in treatment, and
- supportive relationships.

Davis (2014) studied five adult women formally diagnosed with ADHD and learning disorders who were successful in either academia or employment. The majority of these women did not receive therapeutic or academic interventions until adulthood, and many struggled throughout school, blaming their own lack of ability. Davis's results documented that these women attributed their success to many previously identified constructs with new revelations in the areas of:

- their experience of the diagnosis,
- any co-occurring diagnoses,
- coping strategies,
- self-perception,
- adaptiveness (adapting to changes) and flexibility,
- early educational intervention,
- motivation, and
- perseverance.

Books and research by Barkley (2012) and Brown (2013) emphasized the important role a child's executive functioning has on successful daily performance. As we have said previously, executive functioning is an umbrella term for many different activities of the brain that orchestrate goal-directed action. Your child's executive functioning helps him or her:

- focus,
- decide what is important,
- set goals,
- use prior knowledge,
- begin action,
- manage time,
- self-monitor,
- use self-control, and
- remain flexible.

When your child has well-developed executive functions, she can maintain output on academic tasks and self-regulate behavior in social situations. It is important to note that your child's executive functioning is not related to her IQ. Many very bright children have dysfunction with their executive functioning. In Chapter 4, you'll gain insight in how to improve some weaker areas of your child's executive functioning.

Executive functioning is a complex process involving various regions of the brain that communicate via neural circuitry. Executive functioning does not depend on the prefrontal cortex in isolation but involves other subcortical areas, including the basal ganglia, amygdala, limbic system, and cerebellum. Some executive functioning difficulties have been associated with abnormalities in the interior prefrontal cortex. Your child's prefrontal cortex is one of the last areas in the brain to mature, which occurs when your child is in his or her late teens to early 20s. As we discussed in our book *The Impulsive, Disorganized Child: Solutions for Parenting Kids With Executive Functioning Difficulties* (Forgan & Richey, 2015), you can support your child's executive functioning by:

- scaffolding support,
- teaching systems of support, and
- sustaining strengths.

Scaffolding support means you provide enough temporary support to help your child perform while executive functioning skills evolve. While your child is in middle school, you may help her manage time by creating a study schedule. As executive functions mature, you'd expect her to take on some of this responsibility.

*When your child understands her strengths and knows how to use them to her advantage or to bypass weaknesses, your child feels more confident and successful.*

Systems of support help executive functioning weaknesses and are typically supports your child learns to create to bypass his weaknesses. For example, your child might learn it is much easier to take a visual picture of information written on the board rather than copy it down.

When a child finds this type of useful strategy, he begins to "own" it and use it as part of an everyday routine.

We are all about helping your child sustain strengths. When your child understands her strengths and knows how to use them to her advantage or to bypass weaknesses, your child feels more confident and successful. Harnessing your child's natural strengths can take a combination of time, energy, and research. For example, John's son loved science, so during the week he researched science experiments they could do at home on the weekend. These ranged from building volcanoes or rockets to visiting the Kennedy Space Center in central Florida. Among other things, creating a strong relationship with his son rewarded John's effort.

# Characteristics That Sabotage Success

Just as there are characteristics that contribute to your child's success, we acknowledge individuals with ADHD often have barriers that interfere with their success. These vary but can occur from mild to severe. Characteristics that sabotage success include impulsivity, low tolerance of frustration, emotional reactivity, explosiveness, defiance, weak time management, lack of organization, and learned helplessness.

As a tuned-in parent, recognize your child's struggles, but don't berate him for them. When you acknowledge the struggle and how it may impact your child, you can help him gain perspective on it and feel understood. Ignoring or suppressing weaknesses does not make them disappear; it simply masks the underlying needs. Therefore, if your child has any significant barriers to using his strengths, we encourage you to continue to educate yourself about ways to strengthen them, work with professionals if necessary, and meet up with other parents who have shared your journey. Through your efforts, you'll see success is possible. We know the journey has ups and downs, and our hope is that you have more ups than downs.

# Inspiration for Your Journey: Others With ADHD Who Have Achieved Success

## *A Look at Those With ADHD Who Have Achieved Success Across Generations*

ADHD occurs across generations, and in every generation, there are many individuals with ADHD who succeed. Successful adults are self-aware of their strengths and weaknesses and then choose jobs that build upon their assets. They also create support systems or have people in their lives who support their weaker areas.

Successful baby boomers with ADHD are found in every profession but are often underserved in receiving appropriate treatment. Kathleen Nadeau (2017) is a psychologist who specializes in girls and adults with ADHD. In her work studying adults age 60 an older, she found that, "As some older adults have come to understand and accept their ADHD they begin to reject the circumstances in which they had lived due to low self-esteem and lack of confidence" (para. 5). These adults have difficulty in areas like task completion, emotional control, time management, remnants of hyperactivity, and social challenges. In spite of those difficulties, many continue to achieve successful lives by taking medication and receiving coaching.

*ADHD occurs across generations, and in every generation, there are many individuals with ADHD who succeed.*

A well-known baby boomer with ADHD is Terry Bradshaw, a former four-time Super Bowl winner and Pittsburg Steelers quarterback. In his 2001 book, *It's Only a Game*, he revealed that since he was a young boy he struggled with ADHD and reading. Although he had struggles as a pro quarterback, structure and passion for his work helped him achieve success.

# Success With ADHD

Dawn Brown, MD, is a member of Generation X. She is a psychiatrist with ADHD who runs an ADHD Wellness Center in Texas. She has taken her experiences as a professional woman with ADHD and used them at a national level to help others. Brown personally understands the impact of ADHD as a potentially debilitating disorder and specializes in providing balanced and supportive information about ADHD through her clinic, website, and Facebook group. As her website noted, she is the "MD with ADHD" (Brown, 2018). ADHD will not prevent your child from becoming a doctor if that is your child's desire. In our work with parents, doctors, lawyers, politicians, and professionals have disclosed they, too, have ADHD.

Nick is a successful adult with ADHD, but he despised going to school. He always sat in the back of the classroom, rarely participated in class discussions, and claimed he never read a book or studied for a test during high school. During his senior year he vividly remembers his dad telling him, "You either go to college and work your ass off for 4 years to get a degree that can give you a nice job or go right to work and work your ass off until you retire." Because school was not his thing, he went to work. His younger years were not easy, as he divorced, was fired from his first and second jobs, and received multiple speeding tickets. At 52, he has been remarried for 17 years and runs his own successful window treatment company. Recognizing his weaknesses, he hired a highly organized business manager who keeps track of the daily operations and allows him to focus on his team of salespeople and installers.

Neil Petersen, a millennial, is a blogger and ADHD advocate who writes about his success. Petersen (2016) credited his mom with helping him learn to cope with ADHD. Specifically, his mom believed in him, advocated for him in school, and helped him pursue his interest. He wrote:

> Because of the large gap many students with ADHD have between their strengths and weaknesses, it's easy for them to end up spending all their time focused on trying to shore up the weaknesses instead of exploring the strengths. This

is really unfortunate because it's the things we like and that we're good at that give us the most pleasure. (para. 13)

Petersen's mom went the extra mile to help him pursue music, which contributed to developing his confidence and shaped his life.

In a 2018 post on her ADHD blog, Drew Dakessian, a millennial, wrote, "When I was born with ADHD, certain life outcomes were automatically stripped from my grasp. Now, it's up to me to determine what kind of life is within my reach—and then find the strength to do the reaching" (para. 6). Her mindset exudes the desire for a successful and meaningful life.

## Success Secrets and Advice From Famous People With ADHD

When thinking about successful people with ADHD, Michael Phelps is at the top of most lists. As the most decorated Olympic athlete of all time, he credits his success to his mom's support in helping him find a passion. Parenting.com (2014) interviewed him and asked, "What do you tell a kid that is discouraged, hasn't found that passion yet or is struggling in school?" He responded:

I have had extreme ups and downs. The biggest thing I learned after I broke my wrist is to never give up. Nothing in life will ever come easy. It depends on how you deal with those obstacles and how you overcome those obstacles. If you can overcome them, you're a stronger person. If you make mistakes along the way, as long as you never make that same mistake again, you're a successful person. (sec. 3, para. 7)

There are many well-known and successful individuals with ADHD. Sometimes the mainstream media suggest a person's success is because of his or her ADHD. You may have heard commentary that Michael Phelps was a successful Olympic athlete because his ADHD allowed him to hyperfocus on swimming, or that Adam Levine is a successful musician because his ADHD lead him to be a risk taker. Although we agree these people with ADHD are successful, we disagree that their success is only because they have ADHD. Any successful person with ADHD had a variety of influential factors, but central to many of their stories is a person who believed in them. This could have been a coach, teacher, relative, parent, manager, or mentor; but someone believed in the child and helped unlock his or her potential.

Some well-known people with ADHD and the area(s) of multiple intelligence we believe were strengths for them include Howie Mandel (TV personality; interpersonal), Adam Levine (musician, TV personality; interpersonal and musical), Michael Phelps (Olympic athlete; bodily-kinesthetic), Ty Pennington (TV host; visual-spatial, bodily-kinesthetic, and interpersonal), Patricia Quinn (doctor; visual-spatial, linguistic, and logical), David Neeleman, (Jet Blue founder; linguistic and logical), Paul Orfalea (Kinko's founder; interpersonal, linguistic, and logical), Wendy Davis (actress; interpersonal and intrapersonal), James Carville (political commentator; linguistic), and Cynthia Gerdes (owner of Hell's Kitchen; visual-spatial and bodily-kinesthetic).

During interviews and online, some famous individuals have shared their ADHD success secrets and advice. Table 2 outlines some of their experiences.

When compared to famous people with ADHD, there are many more successful people with ADHD who are not well known. We have worked with doctors, journalists, musicians, businessmen, lawyers, entrepreneurs, tradespeople, and athletes with ADHD who also have children with ADHD. In discussing their ADHD, many of these professionals attribute their success to having a parent who believed in them and supported them in following their passion. They also discuss their grit, or the ability to stick with something and persevere until it is obtained.

We'll leave you with this thought. Dr. David Kirby (2008) studied 30 young people, ages 14–25, with ADHD and reported that they were more entrepreneurial than peers without ADHD. He also

Table 2
Well-Known Individuals' Real-Life Experiences With ADHD

| Name | Occupation | Success Secrets | Advice |
|------|-----------|-----------------|--------|
| Simone Biles | Olympic gymnast | "I definitely notice a difference in my training when I'm not getting enough sleep. When I'm tired, I have less energy and it's a lot more difficult to stay focused. I need sleep to rest my mind, restore my muscles and to prepare me to compete at the highest level" (as cited in Starr, n.d., para. 1). | "Having ADHD, and taking medicine for it is nothing to be ashamed of [. . .] nothing that I'm afraid to let people know" (Biles, 2016). |
| David Blaine | Magician, illusionist, and endurance artist | "I think magic . . . is pretty simple. It's practice" (as cited in Goalcast, 2017). | "We all have the ability to perform magic, to endure, to push ourselves beyond our limits, if we have the patience and the resilience" (as cited in Mbe, 2017). |
| Jim Carrey | Actor and comedian | Carrey attributes his crazy, clownish personality to his ADHD. He managed to camouflage his difficulties by being the class clown because it was very difficult for him to be himself (Dwyer Family Foundation, 2016). | "So many of us choose our path out of fear disguised as practicality. What we really want seems impossibly out of reach and ridiculous to expect, so we never dare to ask the universe for it. . . . You can ask the universe for it" (as cited in MulliganBrothers, 2014). |
| Jim Caviezel | Actor | During filming of *The Passion of the Christ*, Caviezel carried the script for the scenes they were filming in his jacket pocket. He also used flash cards and audio files so that he could memorize his lines (JimCaviezel.us, 1998–2017). | He learned to use what makes him different to find his talent and says you can, too. |
| Scott Eyre | Baseball player | Eyre uses technology for organization, leaves himself sticky notes, and took his medicine every day before his games (Redfearn, 2017). | "If I had one wish, I'd wish I could go back to high school and take my medication every day. I could have accomplished so much more. But the more I learn now, the more I can get out to parents" (as cited in Redfearn, 2017, para. 21). |

*Table 2, continued*

| Name | Occupation | Success Secrets | Advice |
|---|---|---|---|
| Howie Mandel | Comedian | "I didn't let ADHD prevent me from achieving my goals and neither should anyone else" (as cited in Bailey, 2009, para. 1). | "Managing symptoms is a lifetime commitment. You have to be willing to experiment. If one thing doesn't work, another will. There are alternatives and there are answers" (Mandel, 2010, para. 10). |
| Roxy Olin | Actress | "Olin takes Adderall, sees a therapist, and uses organization and time-management strategies to keep her symptoms in check" (Shoot, 2011, para. 3). | "I've learned at this point in my life that ADHD is a part of who I am. You don't have to keep your ADHD a secret" (as cited in Shoot, 2011, para. 3). |
| Ty Pennington | TV host, model, set designer | "Pennington admits that ADHD hurt his confidence and his belief in his own abilities, but he found success by pursuing art, design, and carpentry" (Edge Foundation, 2017, para. 6). He said, "It's about the joy of doing things for others . . . random acts of kindness can restore your faith in people" (as cited in TyPennington.com, n.d. para. 6). | "As an adult with ADHD, I know, firsthand, the importance of understanding and treating ADHD. I believe if I'd been diagnosed and treated earlier, I would have struggled less as a child" (as cited in Savage, 2008, para. 3). |
| Michael Phelps | Olympic swimmer | Phelps said failure and setbacks are beneficial, "for they help to fuel him" (Poirier-Leroy, 2016). | "If you want to be the best, you have to do things that others aren't willing to do" (as cited in Poirier-Leroy, 2016). |
| Will Smith | Actor and singer | Smith had trouble focusing enough to read as a child and now he reads more via audiobooks. | "Fail early. Fail often. Fail forward. Failure is a massive part of being able to be successful" (as cited in Mejia, 2018). |
| Justin Timberlake | Grammy Award-winning singer | Timberlake uses humor to deal with the stress that comes along with having OCD and ADHD. | "If you're a young person . . . being called weird or different . . . I'm here to tell you that your critics do not count. Their words will fade, you won't" (as cited in Jang, 2015, para. 5). |

reported that they had a more right-brain learning preference, so they often asked if there was a better way of doing things, challenged routine and tradition, were reflective, viewed issues from a different perspective, realized there may be more than one right answer, saw mistakes as part of the road to success, and had the ability to focus on the broad perspective. Although the study had limitations, such as only including students in a marketing program and not having matched samples, it provides evidence that your child may have an entrepreneurial spirit waiting to be unlocked.

## CONSIDER THIS

1. A large part of your child's success may come from your belief in her. Besides you, who believes in your child?

   _____

   _____

2. Did you relate to any of the advice from famous people with ADHD?

   _____

   _____

3. Your child's potential is waiting to be unlocked. What is your next step?

   _____

   _____

# Chapter 2

# Dream Big, but Realistically

## You Make a Difference

Sometimes you have to let go of the picture of what you thought life would be like and learn to find joy in the story you are actually living.

—Rachel Marie Martin

Think back to when you first learned you were pregnant with your child. Or if you adopted your child, remember when you first learned there was a child for you. Weren't you excited? We are both parents, and as soon as we learned about our children, we started dreaming about them. Like us and many parents, your first dreams about your child were likely about gender and physical appearance. "Will it be a boy or girl?" "What color eyes will our baby have?" "Will our baby look like me?" Then, your dreams likely shifted to how excited the family will be about the baby, followed by dreams about school and careers. Dreaming about your child's future was fun and full of hope and promise.

However, one day you learned that your child has ADHD. When this occurred, you may have felt that your dreams for your child were shattered—or at least rearranged. You may have felt like your child's future was going to be an uncertain tangle of treatments, therapies, tutoring, and challenges. This is a typical reaction to an ADHD diagnosis. But to borrow a lyric from the Casting Crowns song "Just Be Held," "Your world's not falling apart, it's falling into place." We encourage you to try to maintain the optimistic perspective that your child's life is falling into place and that potential is there. Potential can be unlocked by staying intentional in your parenting. As your child's parent, you make a difference. Your investment of time, energy, emotion, and finances will shape your child into her future self.

## CONSIDER THIS

Today, what is your dream for your child?

_____

_____

_____

We encourage you to dream big, but realistically, for your child. This means your child has a promising future in which to live an independent, happy, and fulfilling life, but, because of ADHD, there are additional hurdles to overcome. When Sam and Danielle's son was born, their dream was that their son would be athletic, play sports, enjoy the outdoors, be an average or better student, and attend a college where he would meet his future wife. Before his first birthday, they opened a prepaid college fund for him and began contributions. Danielle dressed him in cute sports clothing adorned with their favorite team's logo while dreaming that her son would one day play for the team. Little did they know that by 10 months, he would require surgery for his chronic ear infections, and by his second birthday, he would need speech and language therapy to address a language delay. At the end of kindergarten, Sam and Danielle's son was diagnosed with ADHD and learning disabilities. He did not enjoy playing many sports, but he tried soccer, football, and baseball. They had him commit to six seasons of baseball before he quit, so that he could learn the cooperation required to be part of a team. During middle school, he was a video gamer. In ninth grade, he was caught smoking marijuana, and by 11th grade, he wanted to drop out of high school. Through lots of prayer, encouragement, and finagling of his school schedule, he graduated from high school. He decided not to attend college. Sam and Danielle's son is happily employed in the trades industry and lives independently. Although the parents' dream did not work out the way they anticipated, they are happy their son is satisfied with his life and that he supports himself. They still dream that one day he will get married.

*Potential can be unlocked by staying*
*intentional in your parenting.*

# Be a Positive Role Model

We all plant seeds. These are the little hints of approval or disapproval we give others through our words and body language. How we interact with people influences their behavior and vice versa. For better or worse, your child is watching and learning from your behavior. Your child is influenced by how you spend your time, use your words, act, treat others, apply your spiritual life, and interact on a daily basis. Regardless if your child is 5 or 15, he or she watches and learns.

If you drink excessively, act moodily, curse like a sailor, or verbally lash out at neighbors or other drivers, there is a high probability that your child will emulate these behaviors. In our work within schools, we often find that when a child is bullying other children, they are usually watching a parent act as a bully.

On the other hand, if you usually speak affirming words and treat others fairly, then your child will likely model these behaviors. Most parents try to demonstrate the golden rule: "Treat others how you want to be treated." We show our kids how to be good citizens, friends, and people. We're not preaching—we are making the point that unlocking your child's potential starts with family. You may have to discuss this with a certain family member who is not being the best role model for your child.

A caveat here is that, even if you model good citizenship and practice good parenting, there will be many times when your child's ADHD will override the good foundation and cause him to act like a menace. Your child's behavior will embarrass you and will even make you question your parenting ability. We know because it has happened to us.

# Strive for a Positive Mindset Toward Your Child

How do you think about your child when she acts like a menace? We want to encourage you to love your child but not the behavior. As we work with children, we often find that they know the best choice to make, but don't always make the best choice. In other words, your child doesn't do what she knows. This is the proverbial gap between knowing and doing, and it is one that many adults with ADHD wrangle with as well.

When Ruth's 8-year-old son was "raging" and going around the house yelling, hitting, and breaking things, he was a little terror whom no family member wanted to be around. He often needed to be physically restrained until he regained self-control. When the episode was over and rational thinking returned, Ruth was able to discuss what happened and give consequences. Her son had remorse and explained,

"It was the 'mean me' that did it." He wanted to control himself but didn't know how.

If you need parenting tools to help yourself and your child, look at Howard Glasser's Nurtured Heart Approach. Glasser created his program from his professional work as a family therapist working with challenging children. The Nurtured Heart Approach is a proactive approach to managing very challenging behavior with the premise that children need to feel safe, seen, and honored. Dr. Leybas Nuno at the University of Arizona studied children diagnosed with ADHD or who were suspected of having ADHD and how they reacted when parented using the Nurtured Heart Approach. Preliminary results found parents reported a reduction in the number of inattention and hyperactivity-impulsivity symptoms in their children when applying the Nurtured Heart Approach (Javier, 2018). You can learn the approach in Glasser's online video-based training at https://childrens successfoundation.com and find his books and videos on Amazon.

Another source of parenting support is through the national center CHADD (Children and Adults with Attention Deficit/Hyperactivity Disorder). It offers an in-person or online parent-to-parent training program that teaches you about ADHD, including treatments, how to create an ADHD-friendly home environment, proactive behavior management techniques, and more. Visit https://chadd.org. ImpactADHD.com also provides a number of resources for parents, including coaching, online seminars, and a blog to provide information about ADHD and support parents. Visit https://impactadhd.com.

# Build a Positive Internal Dialogue

We all have dialogue running through our minds—all of the messages we receive, both positive and negative. Whichever messages we hear the most about ourselves often become who we believe we are. As parents we can recognize what is right in our child and should affirm that. If you have read the book or seen the movie *The Help*, you may remember the maid and nanny Aibileen telling 4-year-old Mae, "You is kind. You is smart. You is important" (Stockett, 2009, p. 521). This contributed to a positive internal dialogue that stuck with Mae. What words could you repeatedly say to your child?

Have you noticed that your child with ADHD often has a negative outlook? She views the glass as half empty rather than half full. Your son may be quick to say, "That's too hard," and push away the work before even reading the directions. Or your daughter may see friends playing outside and say, "They don't like me. They always leave me out." She doesn't seem to recall being invited to the group sleepover last weekend.

*Whichever messages we hear the most about ourselves often become who we believe we are.*

Dr. Daniel Amen, psychiatrist and author of the book *Healing ADD* (2013), described feelings like this as ANTs, or Automatic Negative Thoughts. These thoughts can be captured, squashed, and pushed out of our minds. Help your child learn to recognize when she feels mad, sad, anxious, or worried and talk about how she feels. For instance, you may say, "Going up to bowl in front of all of the people at the tournament seems to worry you. Tell yourself, 'Go away worries. I've practiced, and I can do this. Negative thoughts, you're out of here!'"

To help teach this technique to your child, Amen's children's book *Captain Snout and the Super Power Questions: Don't Let the ANTs Steal Your Happiness* (2017) is a great resource. Most young children enjoy being read to and learning from books. Your child will relate to the characters and learn how she can develop her own ANTeater. Then, practice this technique within your home and family.

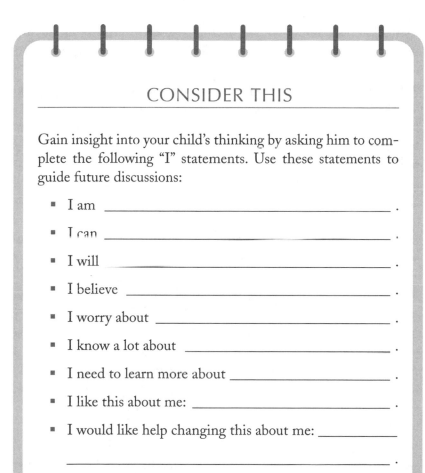

## CONSIDER THIS

Gain insight into your child's thinking by asking him to complete the following "I" statements. Use these statements to guide future discussions:

- I am _____.
- I can _____.
- I will _____.
- I believe _____.
- I worry about _____.
- I know a lot about _____.
- I need to learn more about _____.
- I like this about me: _____.
- I would like help changing this about me: _____

  _____.

# Foster Resilient Thinking and Stress Management

In our fast-paced and technology-filled lives, stressors are practically everywhere you turn. Helping your child develop protective factors that boost his immunity to succumbing to negative impacts of stress is one of the most important things you can do for him. In many cases, the way your child thinks about himself and how he views a situation have a huge impact on the outcome of that situation. You can foster resilient thinking and flexibility in your child to help buffer today's stressors.

Simply put, think about resiliency as a person's ability to be knocked down, get back up, and keep on going. A resilient child is a problem solver who rolls with the punches and takes things in stride. In *Raising Resilient Children*, Brooks and Goldstein (2001) wrote that resilient children "have developed the ability to solve problems and make decisions and thus are more likely to view mistakes, hardships, and obstacles as challenges to confront rather than stressors to avoid" (p. 5). Your child won't automatically view disappointments and mistakes that way. For most children with ADHD, this takes years of maturity and practice.

Some children with ADHD are very rigid in their daily schedule or thinking. If this describes your child, it may be a way she copes with the world. Structure and predictability are ways some children maintain control over their environment. When things don't go the way your child planned, she may not have the coping skills to deal with the change and will need your support. Some supports include helping your child plan an alternate activity, talking her through what the change will entail, giving her time to prepare for the change, or reminding her to breathe, go to a quiet place, or listen to music.

It's important to gradually introduce change into your child's world while teaching skills to handle the changes. When our own children were young, trying to plan ahead to give our children advance warnings about any impending changes was a constant challenge. We became parenting pros at giving our kids a 10-minute warning that change would be coming, a 5-minute warning, a 2-minute warning, and a final 1-minute warning. This prepared them to mentally start adjusting their thinking to the impending change. We really knew this strategy was working when they started using this technique when playing with their siblings.

Of course, life throws us curves, and changes can be so unexpected that you do not have time to mentally prepare your child. Perhaps the flight you're supposed to be on is cancelled, a friend gets sick and can't come over, or the McDonald's ice cream machine is out of service. When these unexpected things happen, turn them into teaching moments. Your child might shed a tear or pout to show disappointment, but when he is back in an even state of mind, discuss the situation. It's important to first recognize how your child may feel before you try to help with the problem-solving process. Begin by stating, "We couldn't control what happened. Sometimes we plan, and our plans don't work out. That was disappointing, and I feel let down." When you recognize how your child feels, he feels validated. Then, move into processing the change. "I'm upset that the ice cream machine was broken. What could we do instead?" This is a better approach than dismissing your child's feelings and saying, "Well, stuff happens. Stop crying and get over it." That does not teach resilient thinking. When you get knocked down it takes practice and support from parents to learn how to get back up and keep going, all within a socially acceptable context.

Some valuable books for children' about worries and resilience include:

- *Is a Worry Worrying You?* by Ferida Wolff (ages 4–8)
- *What Do You Do With a Problem?* by Kobi Yamada (ages 4–8)
- *The Girl Who Never Made Mistakes* by Mark Pett and Gary Rubinstein (ages 4–8)
- *Bounce Back: How to Be a Resilient Kid* by Wendy L. Moss (ages 8–12)

# Never Lose Faith

One thing we repeatedly hear from the families we work with is that kids with ADHD often let their parents down with their behavior and performance. Our kids are consistently inconsistent. This is, in part, because ADHD is a disorder that causes many individuals to underperform. Perhaps you or family members have thought your child is lazy. ADHD can also be a disorder of motivation. In some of his lectures, ADHD expert Russell Barkley suggested that ADHD is more of a motivation deficit disorder because children with ADHD often don't have the stick-to-it-ness or drive to sustain action toward a goal (CorePathway, 2013). Many lack what we call willpower or persistence—the ability to maintain a self-disciplined course toward their goals.

Learning disabilities expert Rick Lavoie wrote *The Motivation Breakthrough: 6 Secrets to Turning On the Tuned-Out Child* (2007). He laid out a plan for parents and teachers to motivate children by matching their motivation style to the type of reinforcement that works for them. For example, if your child is motivated by prestige, then you post her work on the refrigerator, grant an honorary title of principal for the school day, or recognize her efforts with a shout-out to grandparents and relatives. On the other hand, if you child is motivated by prizes, then your child can earn rewards for good behavior, grades, or obtaining goals. The other types of motivation styles include praise, projects, power, and people.

Never lose faith when your child seems unmotivated, but instead, strive to create external support systems to help keep your child on track. Match your child's motivation style to what gets and keeps him going in a positive direction. The investment of your time will pay off in the future.

When we work with teens, we ask them two questions that you may want to ask your child. First, "What motivates you to do well in school?" Answers will vary but may include: "To go to a good college." "So I can earn more money from my report card." "So I don't lose my phone." "To get good grades." "So I don't get in trouble." "I don't know." If needed, you can follow up with additional questions. For instance, when a teen answers, "I don't know," we may say, "You know, a lot of teens are not sure what motivates them to do well in school. Are you satisfied with your grades? What does earning a good grade mean to you?" The idea is to help teens develop some self-reflection because sometimes they are just going through the motions and attending school because that is what kids do. They go to school and get graded without really thinking about it. You can help your child reflect on the value of grades.

# Dream Big, but Realistically

The second question we ask is, "Who controls how well you do in school?" The answer we hope to hear from teens is "Me" or "I do." Sometimes teens answer with "My teacher" or "My parents." If your teen responds with an answer besides "Me," this implies your child has a weak locus of control. That is a psychological term that is related to the degree to which your child believes she has control over the outcomes of events in her life. In other words, if your child takes a test and earns a failing grade, the child with a weak locus of control believes it was the teacher's fault for not teaching the content or for making the test too hard. The child who has a strong locus of control will take ownership and realize she did not sufficiently prepare for the test. We want our kids to have a strong locus of control and believe their actions influence the outcome. They are not passive participants in life. Your child's actions and efforts influence the outcomes.

*We want our kids to have a strong locus of control and believe their actions influence the outcome.*

Discuss your child's locus of control with him. If you ask, "Who controls how well you do in school?" and your child responds with, "I do," then discuss how that is a good mindset to maintain. You might say, "I agree. We control a lot of our day and destiny because the effort we put into what we do has an effect on what happens." If your child has a weaker locus of control by answering, "My teacher," then explain what he is implying. You might say, "Actually, that may not be the case. Although your teacher assigns the grades, it's your effort that determines how well you perform and the type of grade you earn. We are in control over many of the things that happen in our lives, and your schooling is an area in which you have a lot of control." Of course, continue to give examples of how your child's effort has paid off in the past. Changing a child's locus of control is a gradual process, so work this into many conversations.

# Know Your Child's Friends

You may have heard the saying, "Show me your friends, and I'll show you your future." It implies your child will only be as good as the company she keeps. When your child is in elementary school, it is fairly easy to keep tabs on your child's friends, but the older your child becomes, the harder it is to know her friends. At some point, your teen will learn how to drive, and then it becomes even more challenging to know your child's friends. Intentionality is necessary to create opportunities to be around when your child is interacting with friends.

Despite these challenges, you can still know your child's friends. Consider these ideas:

- Allow friends to come to your home to socialize.
- Plan outings, such as driving your child's friends to a ball game. Then, you can talk with your child and her friends in the car.
- Permit your child to have one friend at a time sleep over.
- If you don't already know your child's friends' parents, call and introduce yourself to make a personal connection.
- Allow your child to invite a friend to dinner.
- If your child's friends are online friends, play the online game with them.

The time spent knowing your child's friends will help you understand the influences your child is experiencing. With this knowledge, you can have conversations to guide your child.

*The time spent knowing your child's friends will help you understand the influences your child is experiencing.*

Latoya's daughter was diagnosed in second grade with the combined presentation of ADHD. In eighth grade, she was into social media, especially Snapchat, which is an app to send short videos or pictures that disappear after a short while. Latoya was on Facebook to monitor her daughter's posts but did not use Snapchat—at least not until the incident. Unbeknownst to Latoya, her daughter's "friends" were daring her to engage in oral sex with a boy. She took the dare and took a Snapchat video of it to prove the act to her friends. One friend took a screenshot and then shared it with other friends on social media. Latoya was stunned, and her daughter was teased and deeply embarrassed. It was a hard lesson for both of them.

# Help Set Realistic Goals

"Mom, I'm going to earn straight A's this quarter." If your child made this statement, you might doubt it right away—not because you don't want it to happen, but because you know that it is an unrealistic goal. Goal setting does not come naturally to most children with ADHD. Start with helping your child set small, manageable, and realistic goals that can easily be obtained because success builds success.

Involve your child through conversations about which goals he feels are important and realistic. You might say, "I need your help. We are spending too much time arguing about you getting out of bed in the morning and being on time to get the bus. We need a change. Which one do you want to work on first?" Assuming your child chooses getting out of bed, you might say, "Okay, what are your ideas for you getting up and out of bed?" Engage your child by giving choices and then asking for his ideas. Share your suggestions, and once you reach an agreement, write it down. Display it in a prominent place.

Some common goals we have seen parents set for children with ADHD include:
- bringing their plate to the sink after dinner,
- remembering to brush their teeth before bed,
- independently getting up and out of bed in the morning,
- laying out school clothes the night before,
- putting away materials after use,
- placing homework into a folder or book bag, and
- feeding or walking the pet.

When your child reaches a goal, celebrate it. As you talk to your child about her success, emphasize how good it feels to achieve a goal. Although you want your child to know you are proud of her, the main message she should receive is the intrinsic reward of accomplishing something independently. When your child misses the mark, don't scold her too harshly, as most of us do not complete tasks with 100% accuracy. Instead, offer encouragement for next time. "This morning must have been an off day for getting out of bed, but you will get another chance tomorrow to show yourself you can do it."

# Teach Work Ethic

Imagine where you would be today if you did not know how to work. We do not mean employability, but rather the ability to put in solid time and effort to achieve something or complete a task. We see many children with ADHD who do not sustain effort on tasks that require persistence. Without the ability to sustain effort and demonstrate work ethic, people underperform. They do not reach their potential. They tend to just get by. As an adult with ADHD, life can be tough if you just get by.

To teach your child the value of hard work, begin by not doing things for him that can be done independently. As a parent, sometimes it is easier to go ahead and do things that our kids should do just to avoid another episode of conflict. Lynn's teen son was responsible for caring for the lawn, but on most occasions, she had to repeatedly remind, nag, and then mandate that he mow the grass. It was exhausting. To avoid the battle, she started mowing the lawn. In addition, she did not replace this responsibility with anything else for him to learn work ethic. He started to develop the entitlement attitude of "Mom will do it for me" and barely wanted to clean up his spills or messes.

Giving children chores is a common way to teach work ethic. However, a 2015 article in *The Wall Street Journal* reported in a survey of 1,001 U.S. adults by Braun Research that 82% of adults reported having regular chores growing up, but only 28% said that they require their own children to do them (Wallace, 2015). If you do not agree with giving your child chores, then consider these activities to teach work ethic:

- work on a project together,
- involve your child in simple home repairs,
- volunteer together,
- read or watch movies about heroes who learned the value of work,
- allow your child to make dinner,
- be the guide on the side as you both complete tasks, or
- bring your child with you on "take your child to work" day, so she can see you working hard.

# Set the Bar High

We began the chapter by asking you to write down your dream for your child. This was a premise for identifying a goal for your child. We realize that most dreams don't occur immediately. Achieving one's dreams takes intentionality, effort, determination, and persistence. Most of the time, it's downright hard or sacrificial work. We believe that with the right external support, joined with a strong intrinsic desire, most children with ADHD can accomplish great things in their lives.

Pole vaulters set the bar high, but when they train, they don't begin by setting the bar at the top. Instead, they use a principle called progressive increase. The progressive increase principle implies the vaulter's load must be increased gradually depending on the vaulter's physical and mental abilities to handle the increase. Think about how you can progressively support your child.

Joanna was a single mom who worked two jobs because her dream for her son with ADHD was to see him earn a college degree. She set the bar high by telling him how, with God, all things were possible. She gave up summer vacations, so he could go to robotics camps and pursue his passion with computers. It was not easy with his ADHD.

Throughout school, he worked with tutors and received accommodations. With the help of scholarships and financial aid, her son graduated from college and now works in the information technology field.

Consider your dream for your child, and, if your child is an adolescent, have a discussion with her about it because sometimes a parent's dream does not align with the child's dream. When this occurs, you may have to reframe your expectations to help your child reach her dream.

# Give a Reputation

Use affirming statements to recognize the good you see within your child and communicate that to your child. "You are a hard worker." "You have a caring heart for others." "Your love for animals is amazing." "You're my number one son." Your young child believes what you tell him. The words we use with our kids have the power to build up or tear down their self-esteem. We believe unlocking the potential in your child with ADHD requires that he hears words that build him up.

## CONSIDER THIS

What positive attributes does your child have that you can recognize? Complete these statements:

My child's positive attributes are: _____

_____

_____ .

## CONSIDER THIS, *continued*

I want my child to become _____

_____

_____ .

I need to tell my child, "You are _____

_____

_____ ."

Start speaking the last statement to your child. It becomes more powerful when your child hears it from more than one person. Is there another family member or adult you need to talk with?

# Involve Your Child

As you embark upon this journey to unlock your child's potential, giving your child an age-appropriate explanation of her strengths may be helpful. Below are sample letters of encouragement we wrote that you can share with your child during your discussion if you wish.

## *Letter for an Elementary-Age Child*

Hello,

Being a kid today can be fun but also tough at times. Always remember that you are important. You have a family that loves and cares about you.

Every person has strengths and weaknesses that come out in learning, friendships, and living. Your parent or an adult who cares about your future completed activities to help identify your strengths. We found out that your greatest strengths are _____ . Together, you'll be doing some cool things to build your strengths and improve any weaker areas. It will be fun, challenging, and worth the effort.

It's something we think you'll enjoy, and building strengths takes time, so enjoy the journey. You are unique, one of a kind, and just the way you are supposed to be.

We're on your side,
Jim and Mary Anne

## Letter for a Teenager

Hello,

The teen years can be tough. There's a lot of academic and social pressure. Always remember that you are important, and your life has a purpose that needs to be discovered. Fortunately, you have a family that loves and cares about you and will help guide you.

Each person has strengths and weaknesses that come out in learning, socializing, and living. Your parent or an adult who cares about your future completed activities to help identify your natural talents and qualities. We found out that your greatest strengths are _____ .Together, you'll be doing some cool things to build your strengths and improve any weaker areas.

This is a journey to help you reach your potential, and, along the way, you'll probably discover your passions in life. It's something we think you'll enjoy, and building strengths takes time, so enjoy the ride. You are unique, one of a kind, and just the way you are supposed to be.

We're on your side,
Jim and Mary Anne

# Dream Big, but Realistically

## CONSIDER THIS

1. What can you do to bolster your child's inner dialogue?

   _____

   _____

   _____

   _____

   _____

2. How well do you know your child's friends? List your child's closest friends.

   _____

   _____

   _____

   _____

3. Does your child have a strong enough work ethic? If not, what can you do to make it stronger?

   _____

   _____

   _____

   _____

# Chapter 3

# Unlocking Your Child's Potential

Genius is 1% inspiration and 99% perspiration.

—Thomas Edison

Your child with ADHD may not be a member of Mensa International, the high-IQ society, but that does not mean your child isn't intelligent. You know your child is smart even if he or she has not taken an intelligence quotient (IQ) test; you just don't know an exact IQ score. As school psychologists, we work with children with ADHD and often evaluate them using an IQ test. In our experiences, many children with ADHD have at least an average IQ score. This means the child's IQ is between 90 and 110. In the United States, the average IQ is 100. Mensa International requires your child to have an IQ of 130 or higher on most tests administered by private psychologists.

Taking an IQ test is only one way to define intelligence, however, and many professionals would argue that an IQ score alone is a very narrow way to define intelligence. Although IQ tests do provide valuable diagnostic information to a psychologist, we don't become too fixated on a single score. Your child is more than a single IQ score. Your child is unique, based on your genetics, and shaped by the home and community in which you live and interact. This combination of nature and nurture gives your child multiple intelligences. Society has traditionally looked at intelligence as a score, but we believe children with ADHD are much more than a single IQ score can capture. They are often outside-of-the-box thinkers with innovative minds. Just think about some of the famous people with ADHD described in Chapter 1. They excel in exceptional ways using their humor, body, hands, and minds. As we have stated, this is why we propose that the intelligence of children with ADHD is best described through the multiple intelligence perspective.

*[Children with ADHD] are often outside-of-the-box thinkers with innovative minds.*

As we noted, psychologist and professor Howard Gardner (1983) developed the theory of multiple intelligences. He described seven intelligences: visual-spatial, bodily-kinesthetic, linguistic, interpersonal, logical, musical, and intrapersonal. Later, in 1995, he added an eighth intelligence, naturalistic. Simply stated, the multiple intelligences theory means that intelligence is too broad of a construct to be measured in one way. This theory of intelligence is useful in describing children with ADHD because our kids are unique in their thinking, energy, enthusiasm, emotions, and learning. We know because we work daily helping children with ADHD.

There is no perfect combination of multiple intelligences that your child should have for success. To unlock your child's potential, it is important to examine your child's multiple intelligences and then foster, build, and enhance his or her natural gifts in the top areas. A child's natural strengths often become passions and careers that propel him through life. Table 3 details how Gardner's (1983, 1995) intelligences, as well as how strengths and weaknesses related to them, may manifest in children. This leads us to the main question: Which of these intelligences does your child naturally possess? Unlocking your child's potential partially rests on identifying her multiple intelligence gifts.

*Table 3*
How Gardner's (1983, 1995) Multiple Intelligences Manifest in Children

| Multiple Intelligence | Description | How Struggles May Appear | How Strengths May Appear | Example Careers for People With This Strength |
|---|---|---|---|---|
| **Visual-Spatial** | These children have the ability to mentally visualize the spatial world in their mind's eye. They think in pictures and images, so they visualize how things fit together, whether mechanical or artistic. | Children struggling in this area may have difficulty thinking in physical space, reading diagrams and charts, navigating, focusing on one task/topic, and/or remembering where they placed things. | Children with strengths in this area may excel at reading maps, solving puzzles, designing, creating, remembering things they see, and/or drawing. | Artist, urban planner, graphic designer, architect, engineer, interior designer, pilot, advertiser, sailor, fashion designer, photographer. |
| **Bodily-Kinesthetic** | These children are physical and enjoy using their bodies to convey feelings or ideas, or they may skillfully handle tools, utensils, or sports equipment. They think in movements and use their bodies, in part or whole, to create, learn, process, and problem solve. | Children struggling in this area may be clumsy and/or have difficulty sitting at desk for a long period, fixing things, and/or following verbal instructions. | Children with strengths in this area may have a keen sense of body awareness, excellent motor skills, and/or strong physical education skills, and be able to make things, build, and/or figure out how things work. | Athlete, dancer, equestrian, massage therapist, personal trainer, physical therapist, mechanic, physician, magician, actor/actress. |

*Table 3, continued*

| Multiple Intelligence | Description | How Struggles May Appear | How Strengths May Appear | Example Careers for People With This Strength |
|---|---|---|---|---|
| **Linguistic** | These children enjoy words. Reading, writing, and vocabulary are all areas in which these children excel. Many enjoy learning languages. They can explain information to others. | Children struggling in this area may have difficulty verbalizing and/or finding and saying answers quickly. | Children with strengths in this area may excel at speaking, arguing/debating, storytelling, writing, spelling, and/or reading. | Lawyer, poet, journalist, librarian, radio/TV host, translator, historian, public relations, politician, writer. |
| **Interpersonal** | These children are people-smart, sociable, compassionate, and enjoy being with others. They are naturally skilled at working with groups or on teams. They have a natural knack for mediation, communication, and negotiation. | Children struggling in this area may have difficulty mixing or working with others, and/or waiting to be called on before answering. | Children with strengths in this area may excel at communication, being a people person, resolving conflicts, group work, and/or organizing social events. | Counselor, public relations, therapist, sales person, administrator, event coordinator, mediator, teacher, coach, nurse, manager, clergy. |
| **Logical-Mathematical** | These children are strong with logic and are powerful thinkers. They have the ability to reason, think in numbers, and identify patterns, and they enjoy making connections among different sources of information. They can reason and are critical thinkers asking thoughtful questions. | Children struggling in this area may have difficulty telling stories, solving problems, following oral directions, and/or reflecting on their own work | Children with strengths in this area may excel at identifying patterns, solving puzzles, and/or completing experiments. | Accountant, math, computer analyst, technician, physician, chemist, financial advisor, inventor. |

*Table 3, continued*

| Multiple Intelligence | Description | How Struggles May Appear | How Strengths May Appear | Example Careers for People With This Strength |
|---|---|---|---|---|
| Musical | These children have a natural ability to understand and use music, sounds, instruments, and voice. They think in sounds, rhythms, melodies, and rhymes. | Children struggling in this area may have difficulty singing in tune and reading music. | Children with strengths in this area may excel at writing music, playing instruments, singing, learning through music, and/or humming and tapping out rhythms. | Music teacher, musician, composer, music therapist, sound engineer, music critic, conductor, singer, choir director. |
| Intrapersonal | These children are self-aware or introspective. They understand who they are and don't often mind being alone. They understand their needs and can reflect on how their decisions have consequences. These children may not always prefer to work alone, but they are keenly aware of their learning preference. | Children struggling in this area may have difficulty with collaboration, group work, and/or communication skills because they do not have insight into their own behavior. | Children with strengths in this area may be self-motivated, independent, intuitive, and/or self-aware, and like their own space. | Self-employed, entrepreneur, therapist, psychologist, researcher, writer, theologian. |
| Naturalistic | These children love nature and being outdoors. They often have a keen ability to spot details about animals, weather, Earth, water, trees, and plants. They relate to animals and enjoy gardening and digging. They think by observing, recognizing, and classifying items in the natural environment. | Children struggling in this area may prefer to be inside, may not want to take care of a pet, and/or may not like getting dirty. | Children with strengths in this area may enjoy nature, outdoors, animals, dirt, and/or camping. | Gardener, florist, farmer, astronomer, nature guide, veterinarian, landscape artist, wildlife officer, armed forces. |

*To unlock your child's potential, it is important
to examine your child's multiple intelligences
and then foster, build, and enhance his or
her natural gifts in the top areas.*

# Multiple Intelligences Profile

We created a Multiple Intelligences Profile based on research involving children with ADHD and learning disabilities. The tool (see Appendix A, p. 236) will help you quickly identify your child's strongest areas from the multiple intelligences. Then, you can use this information to create or engage in activities or experiences that build these strengths. If both parents are involved, try rating your child independently and then comparing notes.

How to take it:
1. Think about your child.
2. Read each item.
3. Circle how each item applies to your child.

How to score it:
1. Add together the numbers you circled in each of the intelligences.
2. Once you have totals, record and graph them on the scoring sheet.
3. Identify and circle the top three scores for your child. These are the three multiple intelligences in which your child excels. If there is a tie, your child may have four or more natural intelligences.
4. Read the rest of this chapter about the activities that you can do to continue to strengthen these areas.

## CONSIDER THIS

Harper is an 8-year-old girl with ADHD Combined Type. Her mom used the Multiple Intelligences Profile and identified Harper's top three areas as naturalistic (20), bodily-kinesthetic (19), and intrapersonal (17). Based on Harper's profile (see Figure 2), her mother researched local opportunities outside of school, such as the 4H Club, Girl Scouts, environmental camps, and an animal rescue group. These all provided opportunities for Harper to be outside and engage in hands-on activities. Ultimately, her mother decided on a local environmental camp that emphasized marine biology. She wants to build Harper's love for the ocean and, in her long-range planning, hopes Harper will consider attending a local high school with a marine sciences environmental program. She envisions Harper having a career as a park ranger, scuba instructor or guide, a member of the United States Coast Guard, or in a job in which she can be outdoors. She feels Harper will do best in a job in which each new workday has a degree of unpredictability and Harper gets to move from place to place.

# Identifying Multiple Intelligence Strengths and Weaknesses

Typically, your child will not excel in all eight areas of multiple intelligence. If you were surprised by the outcome of your child's scores, that's okay, too. Your child's multiple intelligence strengths are developing and will likely influence each other. But now that you have identified your child's top multiple intelligences, continue to strengthen those because they may be the areas where your child finds his or her passion or future career. As you continue reading, you'll find activities to build your child's top intelligences.

Keep in mind that the purpose of identifying your child's top multiple intelligences is not to exclude the other intelligences. Multiple intelligences occur and interact together. Just because your child has

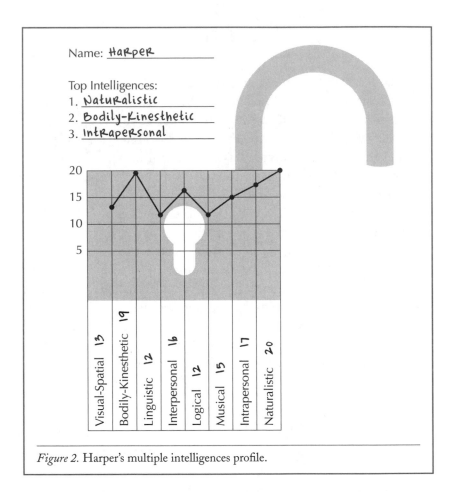

Name: HaRpeR

Top Intelligences:
1. NatuRalistic
2. Bodily-Kinesthetic
3. IntRapeRsonal

Visual-Spatial 13
Bodily-Kinesthetic 19
Linguistic 12
Interpersonal 16
Logical 12
Musical 15
Intrapersonal 17
Naturalistic 20

*Figure 2.* Harper's multiple intelligences profile.

noticeable strength in one area does not mean that he or she should be taught primarily using that form of intelligence. For instance, if your child excelled at bodily-kinesthetic intelligence, you would not want to try to convince your child's teacher that your child must only be taught using hands-on activities. Instead, you may want to support the teacher in using activities to further enhance your child's bodily-kinesthetic talent and use it to build other strengths. Even within her areas of strength, expect your child to struggle with some activities. The struggle is part of the learning process as you help stretch your child's capabilities. Furthermore, children who have experienced repeated failures and have low self-esteem may need more coaxing to develop their strengths. These children often want to give up when tasks require ongoing mental effort.

For each intelligence, the following sections include:

1. further background information to broaden your understanding of the area,
2. examples of how strengths and weaknesses may appear in your child, and
3. a chart of suggestions for strengthening the area and additional resources for leveraging technology.

## Visual-Spatial Intelligence

Visual-spatial intelligence is the ability to accurately perceive the visual world and to visualize how items fit together or relate. Visual-spatial intelligence deals with shapes, patterns, designs, and color. It includes our capacity to visualize, dream, and imagine. Our visual perception is processed in the occipital lobe at the back of the brain.

Children with strengths in this area can mentally visualize the spatial world in their mind's eyes. Children with strong visual-spatial intelligence may excel at drawing, building, sculpting, creating with LEGOs, throwing a ball, or playing visual-spatial computer games, such as *Minecraft* or *Roblox*. When combined with bodily-kinesthetic intelligence, these children may excel at sports. See Table 4 for a list of activities to consider if you want to develop or enhance your child's visual-spatial intelligence.

If your child has weaker visual-spatial abilities, you may notice that she may not enjoy building toys, creating art, or trying to understand maps. She may have difficulty with math. Some children with ADHD are very disorganized because they may not have a strong internal visual map of where to put their belongings.

*Table 4*

Activities for Strengthening Visual-Spatial Intelligence

| Activities | |
| --- | --- |
| ❑ Use imagination magnets<br>❑ Create your own business card<br>❑ Build with K'Nex<br>❑ Build LEGO sets<br>❑ Learn origami<br>❑ Build with PicassoTiles<br>❑ Make and edit videos<br>❑ Play *Minecraft*<br>❑ Volunteer to take photos or sell them on websites<br>❑ Join or start a photography club<br>❑ Play MightyMind game<br>❑ Build with Lincoln Logs<br>❑ Play Busytown game<br>❑ Visit a corn maze<br>❑ Play the Labyrinth game | ❑ Play the Tonga Island board game<br>❑ Create your own mazes<br>❑ Create a personal logo<br>❑ Draw with Crayola Light-Up Tracing Pad<br>❑ Watch videos about creating tessellations<br>❑ Create a mural<br>❑ Visit art galleries<br>❑ Play *Tetris*<br>❑ Play Tangram or spatial puzzles<br>❑ Play *I Shot the Serif* to learn font styles<br>❑ Join a graphic design club<br>❑ Use Perler beads to create designs |
| Leveraging Technology | |
| SonicPics—digital storytelling<br>iMovie—video editing<br>Roblox—user-generated online gaming platform<br>Dragon Shapes—tangram shapes app | |

## *Bodily-Kinesthetic Intelligence*

Bodily-kinesthetic intelligence is the ability to use our bodies to express ideas and feelings in a gross or fine motor manner. Multiple regions of the brain are responsible for coordination, including the cerebellum, cerebrum, and the corpus callosum. These areas allow for voluntary muscle movement, coordination of movement, posture, balance, and equilibrium.

Children with strengths in this area are good at using their body to convey feelings, ideas, or handle objects. Children with strong bodily-kinesthetic intelligence are often referred to as hands-on learners. They enjoy doing things such as science labs, creating, digging, or playing sports. In the classroom, they prefer to move about, jump, sing, and role-play. See Table 5 for a list of activities to consider if you want to develop or enhance your child's bodily-kinesthetic intelligence.

If your child has weaker bodily-kinesthetic abilities, you may notice that she may not excel at coordination and, therefore, may appear awkward in dance, playing sports, or running. Children with ADHD who are weak in this area may have difficulty sitting for extended time periods.

*Table 5*
Activities for Strengthening Bodily-Kinesthetic Intelligence

| Activities | |
|---|---|
| ❑ Participate in gymnastics<br>❑ Create a friendship bracelet<br>❑ Read *Kids Weaving: Projects for Kids of All Ages* by Sarah Swett<br>❑ Play Twister and Sight Word Twister<br>❑ Join a drama club<br>❑ Take a woodshop class in school<br>❑ Plan and participate in scavenger hunts<br>❑ Learn carving or whittling<br>❑ Construct a model car, boat, plane, tank, etc.<br>❑ Play charades<br>❑ Play sports | ❑ Build using premade construction kits<br>❑ Use the app Rhythmic Clap and Tap for Spelling & Memorization<br>❑ Visit trampoline parks<br>❑ Learn to rock climb<br>❑ Play hook ring toss game or cornhole<br>❑ Ride a bike or learn to ride a unicycle<br>❑ Volunteer to help fix things<br>❑ Complete a build-your-own-computer kit<br>❑ Build your own stilts and learn to walk on them |
| **Leveraging Technology** | |
| GoNoodle—movement and mindfulness<br>Motion Maze—interactive treasure hunt through a maze<br>Kids Yoga—app for yoga poses<br>NFL Play 60—football-themed fitness app | |

## Linguistic Intelligence

Linguistic intelligence relates to your child's ability to use language to communicate, convince, and explain. Our language develops on the left side of the brain. Broca's area and Wernicke's area are the parts of the brain involved in language. Broca's area is most responsible for production of speech, whereas Wernicke's area is most responsible for understanding language, whether the language is spoken, written, or gestured.

Children with advanced linguistic intelligence enjoy words. Your child may have a strong vocabulary, enjoy writing, like to read books, remember quotes and sayings, and may speak two or more languages. Those with strengths in this area are usually good at telling stories. See Table 6 for a list of activities to consider if you want to develop or enhance your child's linguistic intelligence.

If your child has weaker linguistic abilities, you may notice that he may not enjoy reading, writing, or lecture-style instruction. Children with ADHD who have weaker linguistic abilities may talk a lot but not have a rich vocabulary or internal thesaurus of words. They may not enjoy learning foreign languages.

*Table 6*
Activities for Strengthening Linguistic Intelligence

| Activities | |
| --- | --- |
| ❑ Write and self-publish a book on Kindle Direct Publishing<br>❑ Give narrated tours at tourist attractions<br>❑ Join a debate club at school<br>❑ Learn a foreign language<br>❑ Start a blog<br>❑ Create a podcast<br>❑ Speak publicly about issues<br>❑ Read aloud (choral, oral, group, interpretive)<br>❑ Listen to audio or video stories<br>❑ Join the school newspaper staff<br>❑ Volunteer at a community theatre | ❑ Volunteer for storytelling at historical locations<br>❑ Take field trips to bookstores, libraries, newspaper offices, etc.<br>❑ Create your own electronic newsletter<br>❑ Write poems<br>❑ Create a menu for a pretend restaurant<br>❑ Play games like Scrabble and Boggle<br>❑ Interview others<br>❑ Create your own greeting cards<br>❑ Memorize the alphabet—backward |
| **Leveraging Technology** | |
| English Idioms Illustrated—app featuring illustrated idioms<br>Words With Friends—multiplayer online Scrabble-like word game<br>Word Magnets—app for sentence building<br>Duolingo—website that teaches foreign languages for free | |

*Interpersonal Intelligence*

There is no one area of the brain that is responsible for social skills. Certain regions within the brain are considered to be the "social brain." They are the amygdala, prefrontal cortex, and posterior superior temporal sulcus. In a most basic explanation, these parts of the social brain allow us to interact with other people. The amygdala is largely associated with fear, the prefrontal cortex with social thinking, and the posterior superior temporal sulcus with social perception.

Children with strong interpersonal intelligence are sociable, outgoing, and compassionate. These children are good at working cooperatively with others, knowing what other people want, being sensitive to others, teaching others, participating in social events, and meeting new people. See Table 7 for a list of activities to consider if you want to develop or enhance your child's interpersonal intelligence.

If your child has weaker interpersonal abilities, you may notice that she may become annoyed when around large groups of people. Other people may easily get on her nerves. Children with ADHD with interpersonal weaknesses perform better playing with only one child at a time and may prefer individual sports or activities.

*Table 7*
Activities for Strengthening Interpersonal Intelligence

| Activities | |
|---|---|
| ❑ Run for student government <br> ❑ Volunteer at a pet shelter or farm <br> ❑ Join a church or religious group for kids <br> ❑ Join team sports <br> ❑ Set up a lemonade stand <br> ❑ Visit nursing homes <br> ❑ Volunteer at the Special Olympics or an Autism Walk <br> ❑ Play Pictionary <br> ❑ Read *25 Ways to Win With People: How to Make Others Feel Like a Million Bucks* by John C. Maxwell <br> ❑ Join a dance team/group | ❑ Create entertaining videos to share with family <br> ❑ Play board games such as Life, Indigo, or Sorry! <br> ❑ Volunteer or try out for dramas and plays <br> ❑ Tutor younger students <br> ❑ Perform puppet shows <br> ❑ Volunteer at a thrift store <br> ❑ Read aloud/recite poetry <br> ❑ Play Project Adventure games <br> ❑ Join a club based on your interests <br> ❑ Start a monthly book club |
| **Leveraging Technology** | |
| Moleskine smart journals notebooks <br> Minecraft—open-ended game <br> Poptropica—multiplayer online role-playing game <br> The Game of Life app—app version of the classic game <br> NASA Kids' Club—online games linked to real missions | |

## Logical Intelligence

Logical intelligence includes the ability to perceive sequence, patterns, and order, as well as to predict, explain, and draw conclusions.

Logical reasoning uses several parts of the brain, including the left parietal lobes, the temporal and occipital lobes, and association cortexes of the brain. These parts of the brain help our thinking and inner thought processes.

Children with strengths in this area have strong analytical reasoning and are powerful thinkers. They are good at strategy games, enjoy math, like science experiments, organize things by category, prefer a rational explanation for things, and wonder how things work. See Table 8 for a list of activities to consider if you want to develop or enhance your child's logical intelligence.

If your child has weaker logical abilities, you may notice that she is more concrete or literal in her thinking and doesn't automatically perceive patterns or relationships. Some children have difficulty with math word problems or reading comprehension.

*Table 8*
Activities for Strengthening Logical Intelligence

| Activities | |
|---|---|
| ❑ Play the board game Lanterns: The Harvest Festival | ❑ Play the Exploding Kittens card game |
| ❑ Learn to code with Tynker | ❑ Find unusual things to measure and calculate |
| ❑ Play the strategy board game Blokus | ❑ Play Mancala |
| ❑ Design a website using Wix | ❑ Join a math club |
| ❑ Use *The Everything Kids' Science Experiments Book* by Tom Robinson | ❑ Learn to play chess |
| | ❑ Play Rummikub |
| ❑ Use a scale to weigh and compare different objects | ❑ Play the classic board game Guess Who? |
| ❑ Perform experiments with the 4M Crystal Growing Experiment Kit | ❑ Create your own language of new written symbols |
| ❑ Watch Kahn Academy math videos | ❑ Play the SET card game |
| ❑ Play Clue | ❑ Play the board game Dragonwood: A Game of Dice and Daring |
| ❑ Learn about the stock market | |

| Leveraging Technology |
|---|
| Move the Turtle—app that teaches programming basics |
| iCircuit—app for experimenting with circuits |
| Monster Physics—educational app |
| Kodable app—programming app for kids |

## Musical Intelligence

The right side of the brain is responsible for much of the processing of music. However, no one area is solely responsible for how the brain processes music because rhythm, naming songs, and reading music are left-brain activities. Salimpoor, Benovoy, Larcher, Dagher, and Zatorre (2011) found that music raises dopamine levels. Because individuals with ADHD often produce less dopamine, this may account for the sense of pleasure and increased arousal they feel when listening to music.

Children with strong musical intelligence understand and use music, sounds, instruments, and voice. These children easily memorize songs, have good rhythm, can tell when a note is off-key, may sing or hum as they work, and are keen to sound changes. See Table 9 for a list of activities to consider if you want to develop or enhance your child's musical intelligence.

If your child has weaker musical abilities, you may notice that he may enjoy listening to music but sing off-key. Your child may struggle with reading music and have little interest in learning to play an instrument.

*Table 9*
Activities for Strengthening Musical Intelligence

| Activities | |
|---|---|
| ❏ Write songs and compose music<br>❏ Listen to music from different historical periods<br>❏ Use rhythm and clapping to memorize math facts and other content-area information<br>❏ Play soft instrumental music during reading or study time<br>❏ Volunteer with a local theatre group<br>❏ Volunteer to teach an instrument to a younger child<br>❏ Rewrite lyrics of your favorite songs<br>❏ Start a band | ❏ Play music games (e.g., Name That Tune)<br>❏ Create original mixes and upload them to YouTube or SoundCloud<br>❏ Create videos of yourself singing and show them to family or friends<br>❏ Learn to play multiple musical instruments<br>❏ Watch music shows, such as *The Voice* or *American Idol*<br>❏ Mix music with a DJ app<br>❏ Sing karaoke<br>❏ Join a dance or singing group |
| **Leveraging Technology** | |
| Audacity—free software for audio editing and recording<br>Maths Rockx—app that teaches multiplication tables through music<br>GarageBand—software for creating music<br>Osmo Coding Jam—coding blocks to make music | |

## *Intrapersonal Intelligence*

In the brain, the frontal lobes contribute to personality, judgment, impulse control, planning, and organizing actions over time. They also help us behave appropriately in social situations. Children with strong intrapersonal intelligence are self-aware or introspective. They understand their strengths, understand what works for them, make good decisions, are intuitive, and are independent. See Table 10 for a list of activities to consider if you want to develop or enhance your child's intrapersonal intelligence.

If your child has weaker intrapersonal abilities, you may notice that she prefers to be around other people rather than being alone. Children with weaker intrapersonal abilities don't always have insight into themselves and may not like to do introspective activities, such as journaling.

*Table 10*
Activities for Strengthening Intrapersonal Intelligence

| Activities | |
| --- | --- |
| ❑ Create a scrapbook<br>❑ Keep a journal or diary<br>❑ Make photo albums, books, slideshows<br>❑ Write out your goals<br>❑ Start a collection<br>❑ Solve brain teasers or riddles<br>❑ Build using clay or Play-Doh<br>❑ Solve jigsaw puzzles<br>❑ Start a blog | ❑ Take a free online learning style inventory<br>❑ Write your own autobiography<br>❑ Rewrite a story from your own perspective<br>❑ Do yoga<br>❑ Visit museums<br>❑ Research family genealogy<br>❑ Read or watch biographies |
| **Leveraging Technology** | |
| Popplet—app for creating mind maps to capture and organize ideas visually<br>Kahoot!—a game-based platform to play, create, and host quizzes<br>Book Creator—app for publishing your own book<br>Doodlekit Kids Website Builder & Maker—a free website builder | |

*Naturalistic Intelligence*

Children with strong naturalistic intelligence love nature and being outdoors. They enjoy animals, camping, climbing in trees, and monitoring the weather. See Table 11 for a list of activities to consider if you want to develop or enhance your child's naturalistic intelligence.

If your child has weaker naturalistic abilities, you may notice your child prefers to be indoors. They may be very sensitive to environmental temperature. Some children with naturalistic weaknesses do not like to go on hikes, on bike rides, or camping.

## CONSIDER THIS

Ethan was entering ninth grade when Mary, his mom, completed the Multiple Intelligences Profile (see Figure 3). She identified his top three multiple intelligence strengths as linguistic (20), logical (19), and musical (18). She explained that, as a toddler, he was very verbal, always had an advanced vocabulary, and talked at a level above his age. He was a voracious reader, was a strong thinker, and had an excellent memory. He started piano lessons when he was 5 and mastered the trumpet when he was 9. Ethan was able to compensate for his weaknesses with his intelligence and intuition throughout his more formative years, but he was diagnosed with ADHD, Inattentive Presentation, at age 10.

*Table 11*
Activities for Strengthening Naturalistic Intelligence

| Activities | |
|---|---|
| ❏ Go geocaching | ❏ Go kayaking, canoeing, or paddle boarding |
| ❏ Care for pets or plants | |
| ❏ Research animal habitats | ❏ Make a bird feeder and go bird watching |
| ❏ Become a junior ranger with the National Park Service | |
| | ❏ Create a terrarium with the Creativity for Kids Grow 'n Glow Terrarium kit |
| ❏ Help at park or playground cleanups | |
| ❏ Start or help with recycling projects | ❏ Start a garden |
| ❏ Volunteer on Earth Day | ❏ Go fishing |
| ❏ Collect natural organisms or rocks | ❏ Explore using Google Earth |
| ❏ Plant a tree | ❏ Go snorkeling |
| ❏ Go camping or kayaking | ❏ Build a treehouse or fort |
| ❏ Do nature experiments (e.g., measure plant growth rates) | ❏ Start an outdoor business |
| | ❏ Watch nature TV shows |
| ❏ Volunteer at a nature center | ❏ Build a bat house |
| ❏ Visit zoos | |
| Leveraging Technology | |
| Geocaching—app for outdoor treasure hunting | |
| Discovery—website and TV channel for Shark Week and other nature-related TV shows | |
| Star Walk—app for stargazing | |
| iBird Yard—app-based bird-watching guide | |

Mary always saw him as making a good doctor, so she had doctor friends mentor Ethan. By simply being around doctors, hearing them use medical jargon, and seeing their lifestyle, he realized he shared the same interests. During his younger years, Mary had Ethan attend local science and music camps. Ethan applied, and was accepted, to a high school medical magnet program. During the summer before his freshman year, he volunteered in a physical therapy office. In high school he planned to join the Health Occupations Students of America (HOSA) club and take on a leadership role in that club. Mary is hopeful that he will continue to work hard and believes he can become a doctor if that is his desire.

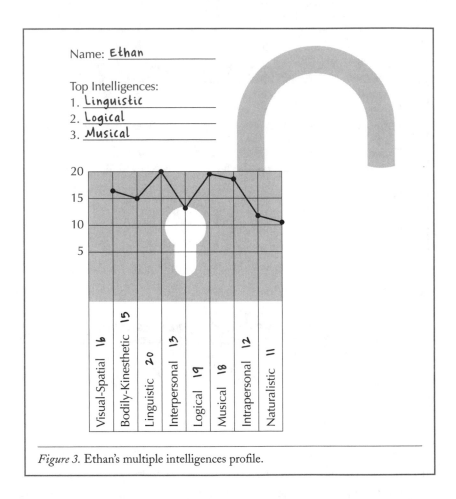

Name: **Ethan**

Top Intelligences:
1. **Linguistic**
2. **Logical**
3. **Musical**

*Figure 3.* Ethan's multiple intelligences profile.

# How Multiple Intelligences Occur in Famous People With ADHD

With your support and a lot of hard work, your child with ADHD has the potential to become the next successful athlete, designer, business owner, politician, artist, comedian, actress, chef, or writer. Just consider the famous people with ADHD working in their multiple intelligence strength areas listed in Table 12. If your child is age 8 or older, consider sharing this information with her.

*Table 12*
Famous People With ADHD Who Display Strength in an Intelligence

| Intelligence | Famous Individual(s) |
|---|---|
| Visual-Spatial | Alexis Hernandez—Chef and reality TV star<br>Ansel Adams—Photographer<br>Cynthia Gerdes—Co-owner of Hell's Kitchen and founder of Creative Kidstuff<br>Dean Kamen—Inventor<br>Frank Lloyd Wright—Architect<br>Leonardo da Vinci—Artist<br>Richard Branson—Founder of Virgin Group<br>Ty Pennington—TV host, artist, carpenter, author, former model<br>Steven Spielberg—Director |
| Bodily-Kinesthetic | Cammi Granato—U.S. women's hockey<br>Andre Brown—Football running back<br>Bubba Watson—PGA Tour pro<br>Channing Tatum—Actor<br>Greg LeMond—3x Tour de France winner<br>Jim Carrey—Actor<br>Michael Phelps—Olympic swimmer<br>Simone Biles—Olympic gymnast<br>Sylvester Stallone—Actor |
| Linguistic | Agatha Christie—Author<br>Dav Pilkey—Author<br>Christopher Knight—Actor and businessman<br>Daniel Koh—American politician and former Chief of Staff to Mayor of Boston<br>Katherine Ellison—Writer<br>Lisa Ling—Journalist<br>Michelle Rodriguez—Actress<br>Richard "Rick" Green—Comedian, satirist, actor, writer |
| Interpersonal | David Blaine—Magician<br>Emma Watson—Actress<br>Howie Mandel—Comedian<br>Jim Caviezel—Actor<br>Margaux Joffe—Consultant and producer<br>Will Smith—Actor |
| Logical | Jamie Oliver—Star chef<br>Paul Orfalea—Kinkos founder |

*Table 12, continued*

| Intelligence | Famous Individual(s) |
|---|---|
| Musical | Adam Levine—Singer<br>Brendon Urie—Singer<br>Chris Webb—Rapper<br>Justin Timberlake—Singer<br>Karina Smirnoff—Professional ballroom dancer<br>Solange Knowles—Singer<br>Zooey Deschanel—Actress/musician |
| Intrapersonal | David Neeleman—Founder/former chairman/CEO of JetBlue<br>Glenn Beck—Political commentator<br>James Carville, Jr.—Political strategist<br>Russell Brand—Comedian, actor, host, author, activist |
| Naturalistic | Sharon Wohlmuth—Award-winning photo journalist |

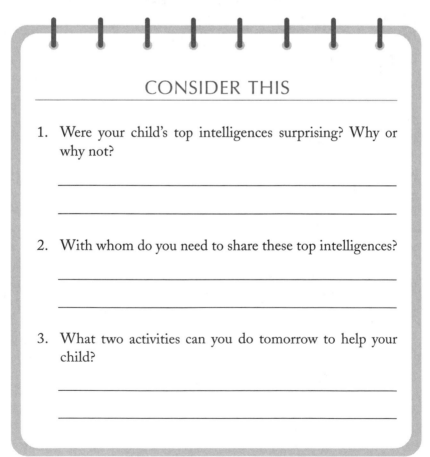

## CONSIDER THIS

1. Were your child's top intelligences surprising? Why or why not?

   _____

   _____

2. With whom do you need to share these top intelligences?

   _____

   _____

3. What two activities can you do tomorrow to help your child?

   _____

   _____

# Chapter 4

# Keys to Success

Sometimes our light goes out but is blown into flame by another human being. Each of us owes deepest thanks to those who have rekindled this light.

—Albert Schweitzer

Hopefully you are feeling positive after identifying your child's natural gifts and talents in the previous chapter. Or, perhaps now that you have gone through the process of really thinking about your child's natural abilities, you may be a bit sad to realize that one of your dreams may not be realistic. Take heart—we are just trying to get you started in the direction of thinking about natural abilities. Your child is a work in progress, and it is possible that he hasn't even been exposed to his strongest talents yet.

Continue to expose your child to the world and provide opportunities for her to find passions. Then, if she wishes, support your child in developing those talents, providing additional motivation if necessary. As we have discussed previously, children who have experienced repeated failures and have low self-esteem may need more coaxing to develop their strengths. Sometimes interest grows stronger as skills improve. In our practice and in our own families, we have found that most children gravitate toward what they do well and actually enjoy doing. Who among us really enjoys doing things we are not good at?

Although you may still have more work to do in helping your child find and develop natural talents, you can still move on and take a look at the 11 keys to success addressed in this chapter (see Figure 4) that are crucial for success in almost any field and for happiness in general. Eight of these are personal characteristics, like motivation, integrity, and emotional regulation. The other three are external conditions that need to be present: appropriate school setting, support systems, and appropriate use of technology, which is intended for parents of older children.

Just being aware of areas that need strengthening is a good place to start. Consider this quote from James Baldwin, American author and social critic: "Not everything that is faced can be changed, but nothing can be changed until it is faced." Like this quote, our hope is that, from the survey included in this chapter, you can identify several areas that should be strengthened in your child to enable him to use his natural abilities to their fullest.

Keep in mind that your child's makeup may not enable him to improve all of the keys to success. For example, organization is one of the keys. People with ADHD often struggle with keeping their personal items and affairs organized. No matter how hard you try, you may be unable to help your child develop organizational skills to your liking. Plan B would be to help him be aware of what needs to be organized in his life and use technology or other people to help compensate for his difficulties. Many successful adults with ADHD credit their spouses or programs or apps, such as Cozi Family Organizer or Google Calendar, for helping them keep track of responsibilities and meet deadlines. Many CEOs with ADHD rely on executive assistants to keep track of the details and organize their days. You can help your child find supports in his environment to help with organization.

---

*Internal Factors*

1. Motivation
2. Emotional stability and behavioral control
3. Integrity
4. Social skills
5. Grit
6. Organization
7. Resilience
8. Resourcefulness

*External Factors*

9. Appropriate school setting
10. Support systems
11. Productive use of technology (primarily for older children)

*Figure 4.* Keys to success.

---

# The Keys to Success Survey

Just as in Chapter 3, we have provided a questionnaire for you to rate your child's characteristics and behaviors. However, on this survey, you are not going to be looking for your child's strength areas, but at weaker areas that could prevent your child from maximizing the natural strengths you identified in the Multiple Intelligences Profile. No one possesses all 11 keys to success, so don't be dismayed if your child shows a number of deficit areas. Your goal is not to overwhelm your child by trying to pick too many weaker areas to address. Some of these abilities come with maturity. Think of your child as a work in progress. Hopefully you will have many years to help your child develop and refine these characteristics needed for success. Many of these skills can be improved through your daily interaction with your child—helping her reflect on situations that have happened, sharing your own experiences, or providing opportunities for growth through experiences. You might even find something you would like to improve in your own life. Then you and your child could work together, which could be a learning and bonding experience for both of you.

The Keys to Success Survey (see Appendix A, p. 241) will help you quickly evaluate characteristics and conditions important for success. Use the results to create or engage in conversations or experiences that strengthen deficit areas. Remember to choose only one or two areas to focus on at a time so as not to overwhelm yourself or your child. Although it may be difficult for you to think about putting one more thing on your plate, helping your child improve these skills can ultimately make your life and hers much easier. If both parents are involved, try rating your child independently and then comparing notes.

How to take it:
1. Think about your child.
2. Read each item.
3. Circle how it applies to your child.

How to score it:
1. Score the survey by adding up the numbers you circled in each of the skill areas.
2. Record and graph the total for each characteristic on the scoring sheet.
3. Identify your child's weakest areas—her lowest scores. Read the rest of this chapter about the activities that you can do to continue to strengthen these areas.

## CONSIDER THIS

Eight-year-old Luis is gifted in his ability to see how things go together. He loves to build and create structures, especially outside in his natural environment. He loves reading and is able to read above-grade-level texts. Writing, however, is a different story. He hates to write and avoids it whenever possible. He is also very easily frustrated and loses his temper if a structure he is building does not turn out as planned or if his writing doesn't look as good as that of his classmates.

His parents completed the Multiple Intelligences Profile (see Figure 5), identifying Luis's intelligences in the following areas: visual-spatial (16), linguistic (20), and naturalistic (18). His parents also completed the Keys to Success Survey (see Figure 6), identifying

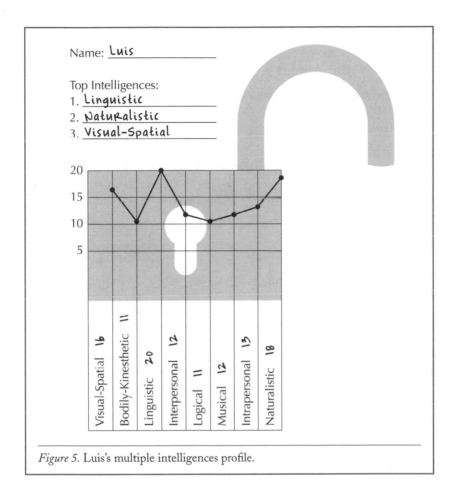

Name: Luis

Top Intelligences:
1. Linguistic
2. Naturalistic
3. Visual-Spatial

- Visual-Spatial 16
- Bodily-Kinesthetic 11
- Linguistic 20
- Interpersonal 12
- Logical 11
- Musical 12
- Intrapersonal 13
- Naturalistic 18

*Figure 5.* Luis's multiple intelligences profile.

deficits in Luis's emotional stability/behavioral control (8), grit (10), and resourcefulness (8).

Luis's teacher and parents agreed that his behavioral control was the most important skill to tackle first because it was causing him the most difficulty in school. His parents met with his teacher to determine triggers for his meltdowns. Luis was embarrassed when he lost his temper in the classroom and was very open to working with his teacher and parents on selecting coping strategies to use when he could feel that he was getting upset. When presented with a coping menu (see Appendix B), he chose to squeeze a small stress ball his teacher

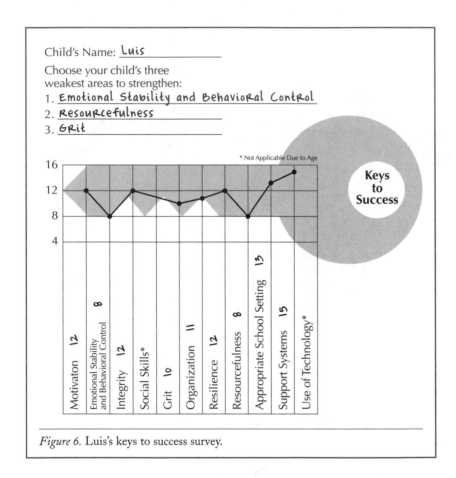

Child's Name: Luis

Choose your child's three
weakest areas to strengthen:
1. Emotional Stability and Behavioral Control
2. Resourcefulness
3. Grit

* Not Applicable Due to Age

Keys
to
Success

| | | | | | | | | | | |
|---|---|---|---|---|---|---|---|---|---|---|
| Motivaton 12 | Emotional Stability and Behavioral Control 8 | Integrity 12 | Social Skills* | Grit 10 | Organization 11 | Resilience 12 | Resourcefulness 8 | Appropriate School Setting 13 | Support Systems 15 | Use of Technology* |

*Figure 6.* Luis's keys to success survey.

gave him, which didn't work out because he was rarely able to find it when he needed it. As an alternative, Luis and his teacher decided he should go quietly to a calm down area in the classroom until he was able to regain control. The first two times he lost his temper, he forgot to go to the calm down corner but did on the third event with a gentle reminder from his teacher. He was encouraged and knew he could get better and better at keeping his behavior under control.

After Luis's behavior was under better control, his parents and teacher decided to address his lack of resourcefulness. His parents brainstormed ways that Luis could receive help with his writing. Luis realized that his phonics skills were getting better and better and agreed to try to first sound out the word that he was trying to spell. He remembered the word wall in his classroom and decided that he could look for the word if he was unable to sound it out, rather than getting frustrated. His teacher also gave him permission to ask another student when he had tried to sound out the word and also checked the word wall. His teacher helped him create a journal folder in which he could keep all of his writings. As Luis began to see the improvement, he was much more willing to focus during writing time. As he matured, he began to see that problems are not stone walls but often have multiple solutions. He gradually came to accept the fact that some days were better than others because of his ADHD symptoms.

# Strengthening Internal and External Keys to Success

Unlike your child's Multiple Intelligences Profile in which you identified your child's strengths and focused on her strongest areas, you should pay attention to your child's weakest areas on the Keys to Success Survey. Remember that these are the characteristics or conditions needed for success in almost any field and are areas you can strengthen in your child. Of course, you will want to continue strengthening stronger areas, but our focus in this chapter is to help you promote growth in areas that might hinder future success. As parents, we want to prepare our children the best we can for the complex future ahead of them. Some tips include:

- Pick only one or two factors to focus on at a time. Some parents like to start with an area in which they think their child has a chance at being successful. Others are up for a challenge and focus on the area that is causing their child the most difficulty, regardless of how daunting it might be to effect change in that area.
- If your child is 8 or older, develop a partnership and involve him, if possible, in developing interventions. Children often

have very good ideas about how to help themselves. If your child buys into the process, the results are usually much better.

- Don't give up on your attempts to help your child after only a few days and abandon your interventions. Often, it takes weeks or longer to see any change, and interventions often have to be tweaked along the way.
- Learn to embrace small improvements. If your child is disorganized and has been all of her life, developing better organizational skills could take years.
- Remember it is a process. If you are moving in the right direction, you and your child are better off than you were yesterday.
- Don't give up. Be resourceful and ask for help when you need it.

To begin helping your child strengthen his weaknesses, for each internal and external key to success, the following sections include:

- background information, including the latest research presented in parent-friendly terms, to give you a broad understanding of the area;
- examples of how weaknesses in the area might appear in children;
- suggestions for strengthening the area;
- additional print and technology resources for further information;
- possible careers for adults with strengths or weaknesses in the area; and
- an example of a person with weaknesses in the area who has improved his or her skills.

Before you read about each key to success in more depth, take note of the following:

- **Executive functioning skills:** Many of the internal keys are considered to be *executive functioning skills*, which are the brain-based skills necessary to get things done. They involve focusing, planning, recalling and using previous experiences in decision making, initiating activities, seeing something through to completion, being flexible when things don't go well, and managing time. Executive functioning abilities are centered primarily in the prefrontal cortex in the frontal lobe with connections to various other parts of the brain. The frontal lobe is sometimes the last area of the brain to mature. Children with ADHD almost always have deficiencies in some, but not all, executive functions. Executive functioning skills are developmental in nature with maturation continuing even into the teen and young adult years. According to Brown (2014), "A study of over two hundred children with ADHD showed that brain networks that support self-management tend not to fully mature in those with ADHD until two to five years later than in most of their peers" (p. 101). Note that some improvement may occur with maturation, but it is still important to be proactive in helping your child develop necessary skills for success. Remember also that change is never easy, so patience and fortitude will be required.

- **Additional resources:** The sections that detail additional resources about each key to success include several books you can read to and with your child. Follow this framework, which includes: (a) reading the book ahead of time to make sure it's appropriate for your child, (b) reading to or with your child and pausing to discuss the book's ideas, (c) discussing how the book's character used the skill or solved a problem, and (d) discussing how the ideas can help in your family or at school.

- **Possible careers:** Keep in mind that, although you have identified deficits in your child, these may be only temporary. Your efforts to improve skills in your child could yield big results, given all of the research that demonstrates the neuroplasticity of the brain (the ability of the brain to change as a result of experience). The sections about possible careers take an optimistic road and first discuss careers that are often filled with people who strongly exhibit the success-related characteristics. Secondly, we highlight career choices for people who continue to be weak in these areas. These lists are merely examples of many possibilities.

# Internal Factors

## *Motivation*

**Background information.** One of the most critical elements in any attempt to change a behavior is motivation, an executive functioning skill involving the will or desire to do something. We will talk about motivation and initiation together because we know that true motivation involves the ability to get started on a task. How frustrated we all have been with good intentions that have no follow through. According to Brown (2013), researchers have been too focused on impulsivity associated with ADHD and not enough on "the emotional problems with *ignition*-chronic difficulties with getting started on necessary tasks and staying motivated to finish what needs to be done" (p. 12). In our experience, some hard-working parents find it incomprehensible that their child with ADHD can't "just do it." A natural tendency is to be negative and critical about the child's lack of willpower, but that rarely results in positive change and can tear down the child, leading to self-loathing and resentment. The best mentors are supportive and encouraging. As Duckworth (2016) observed, "Longitudinal studies tracking learners confirm that overbearing parents and teachers erode intrinsic motivation" (p. 107).

As parents strive to improve motivation, they should understand that doing so may require significantly more effort than expected. Key to succeeding is having some understanding of the neurological components of ADHD and that a child's lack of motivation and initiation is related to how he or she is wired. Barkley (1997) noted that "frontal lobe underactivity, particularly under reactivity to events" (p. 290) is evident in PET scans of children with ADHD. A child may know what to do but may be unable to translate that knowledge into action, as though "there has been a breakdown in the sending and receiving of commands" (Forgan & Richey, 2015, p. 157).

> *One of the most critical elements in any attempt to change a behavior is motivation, an executive functioning skill involving the will or desire to do something.*

Human behavior related to motivation is built on rewards. If you go to work, you earn a paycheck. If your child performs on grade level, she will be promoted to the next grade level. Research has shown that children with ADHD aren't as receptive to long-term rewards as other children and often work better when a deadline is looming, or a reward is imminent. PET scans have revealed that "chemicals that activate reward-recognizing circuits in the brain tend to bind on significantly fewer receptor sites in people with ADHD" compared to other people (Brown, 2013, p.14).

Parents often wonder how children with ADHD can be so focused and motivated to complete tasks they enjoy and appear so apathetic about completing tasks that are obviously important but not interesting to them. Whatever they are interested in is inherently satisfying to them. They are stimulated and rewarded by the time they spend on the activity. Video games are one area in which we see children, especially boys, with ADHD having an intense interest. Video games provide fast-changing images and immediate results. For some children with ADHD, video games provide an alternate world in which they can find the success and satisfaction they can't find in real life. For other children, building with LEGOs is intriguing. Sometimes we can try to determine what it is about the activity that is so rewarding and try to incorporate some aspect of that into other tasks. For example, perhaps it is the immediate gratification of designing a LEGO structure or the hands-on aspect that is rewarding. If you have a younger child who is reluctant to start math assignments, try incorporating manipulatives to see if it makes the math assignment more rewarding or help your child see how math skills can be useful in constructing LEGOs.

Children's motivation to do things on their own is variable. Some are fiercely independent from an early age, whereas others are quite dependent on others. As parents, we want to encourage children to do things for themselves as soon as they are able. That independence boosts self-esteem and internal motivation. When we swoop in and take over for our children, we are saying that they are not capable of doing things for themselves. We probably all know of cases in which parents are so involved in their child's homework that they are basically doing more of it than the child. In that case, it is important to differentiate between what is the child's responsibility and what is the parent's. The parent is responsible for providing a place conducive to doing homework and perhaps deciding when the child should start the homework. The child is responsible for actually doing the homework and asking for help when needed. Table 13 describes the developmental guidelines for task initiation. You can see that between ages of 6–12, children start to compare themselves to others, which can be a source of inferiority that can contribute to lack of motivation.

**How weaknesses in motivation appear in children.** A child with low motivation isn't a self-starter and doesn't seem to have an interest in accomplishments. He needs prodding to start activities and rarely starts them on his own. Any successes he achieves may not be particularly meaningful. There are many factors to consider that can impact motivation. Here are some questions to ask yourself:

- **Is your child possibly depressed, anxious, or oppositional defiant?** It is important to address any of these with a mental health professional, such as a therapist or psychologist.
- **Could your child's motivation be related to a physical condition, such as anemia or lack of sleep?** If you have concerns about physical health, get your child checked out by a doctor. If your child does not get good sleep, even after adjusting bedtime and ensuring no access to electronic devices in the bedroom, consult your child's doctor.

*Table 13*
Guidelines for Task Initiation Development

| 2–3 years | • Begin to realize they have control over actions (Teeter, 1998). |
|---|---|
| 2–6 years | • Initiative begins to develop (LeFrancois, 1995). |
| 6–12 years | • May judge their competence based on comparison to peer group; sense of inferiority may develop (Hébert, 2011). |

*Note.* From *The Impulsive, Disorganized Child: Solutions for Parenting Kids With Executive Functioning Difficulties* (p. 161), by J. W. Forgan and M. A. Richey, 2015, Waco, TX: Prufrock Press. Copyright 2015 by Prufrock Press. Reprinted with permission.

- **Does your child have the skills needed to complete an activity?** If she needs to study for a test, does she have the academic skills to understand the material? If not, address those issues through tutoring or additional help from the school.
- **Is your child a perfectionist?** Some children are reluctant to start tasks because they know the results won't be perfect. Resources are included at the end of this section for helping your child manage perfectionism. If perfectionism significantly impacts his performance, cognitive behavioral therapy with a licensed therapist or psychologist may be needed.
- **Does your child fear failure?** Sometimes without realizing it, parents are too critical and set expectations that are too high. Some children are very perfectionistic and need to recognize that failure can just be a stepping stone to figuring out how to do something better.
- **Does your child have "learned helplessness," a term to describe children who have learned that it is easier to wait for someone to do something for them than to do it themselves (Hiroto & Seligman, 1975)?** If so, it will be important to step back and make sure you are not doing things for your child that he can do independently.
- **Does your child have a poor concept of time?** Some children have no understanding of how much time an activity takes so they don't plan enough time to get something done. It can be helpful to have them time themselves doing different activities, so they are aware of how much time an activity requires.

Clocks, timers, and schedules can help children stay on track. Figure 7 is an example of a task estimation chart that children can use to understand how long specific activities take.

- **Is your child easily overwhelmed by the number of things to do or the complexity of the task?** If so, simplify the schedule and break large tasks down into small, manageable units.

**Strategies for strengthening motivation.** In our practice, we find nothing kills motivation like negativity and the feeling that the task is insurmountable. Motivation can be enhanced when a person:

- identifies with a goal or can see the personal benefit,
- sees that hard work produces results and that the goal is attainable, and
- has supports and encouragement.

Parents often tell us that their child is lazy when the child is actually completely overwhelmed and doesn't know where to start. If you help your child learn to set goals and then break a large task down into small steps that the child knows she can successfully complete, she is much more likely to embrace the challenge. Children often take their cues from their parents, so have confidence that you and your child can work as a team to improve initiation and completion of nonpreferred tasks. Table 14 is a list of strategies for strengthening motivation in your child.

**Resources for strengthening motivation.** Books for children include:

- *The 7 Habits of Happy Kids* by Sean Covey (ages 4–8)
- *Reaching Your Goals* by Robin L. Silverman (ages 10 and up)
- *The Ultimate Book of Inspiring Quotes for Kids* by Michael Stutman and Kevin Conklin
- *Attitude: Discover the True Power of a Positive Attitude* by Ace McCloud
- *Keys to Success for Kids: 2.0* by Caleb Maddix

| Task | My Predicted Time | My Actual Time |
|---|---|---|
| Showering and drying off | 5 minutes | 9 minutes |
| Brushing teeth | <1 minute | 2 minutes |
| Dressing | <1 minute | 2 minutes |
| Fixing hair | <1 minute | <1 minute |
| Socks and shoes | 1 minute | 3 minutes |

*Figure 7.* Sample task estimation chart. From *The Impulsive, Disorganized Child: Solutions for Parenting Kids With Executive Functioning Difficulties* (p. 143), by J. W. Forgan and M. A. Richey, 2015, Waco, TX: Prufrock Press. Copyright 2015 by Prufrock Press. Reprinted with permission.

Books for adults include:

- *A New Understanding of ADHD in Children and Adults: Executive Function Impairments* by Thomas E. Brown
- *Empowering Youth With ADHD: Your Guide to Coaching Adolescents and Young Adults* by Jodi Sleeper-Triplett
- *50 Tips to Help Students Succeed: Develop Your Student's Time-Management and Executive Skills for Life* by Marydee Sklar
- *Smart But Stuck: Emotions in Teens and Adults With ADHD* by Thomas E. Brown
- *The Motivation Breakthrough: 6 Secrets to Turning On the Tuned-Out Child* by Rick Lavoie
- *NurtureShock: New Thinking About Children* by Po Bronson and Ashley Merryman
- *Helping Students Motivate Themselves: Practical Answers to Classroom Challenges* (Vol. 2) by Larry Ferlazzo
- *Mind in the Making: The Seven Essential Life Skills Every Child Needs* by Ellen Galinsky

*Table 14*
Strategies for Strengthening Your Child's Motivation

| Characteristics | Activities to Strengthen Motivation |
|---|---|
| Appears to have no interests | 1. Expose your child to new experiences through family activities or with friends.<br>2. Help your child complete an interest inventory. Plenty of examples can be found online (see https://www.pinterest.com/explore/student-interest-inventory for many ideas).<br>3. Determine if there is an interest you and your child could explore together.<br>4. Review the strengths from your child's Multiple Intelligences Profile and generate ideas related to her strengths. |
| Doesn't initiate action or start activities unless it is an area of interest | 1. Help your child develop a schedule that includes work before play (e.g., half an hour of reading before a half an hour of video games). Be aware of his need for breaks and opportunities to release pent-up energy.<br>2. Some children benefit from "priming the pump," or getting in the right mindset by completing an example first.<br>3. Make sure your child's work area is conducive to starting an activity. Let her help set up a study area free of clutter and distractions.<br>4. Beginning at an early age, give your child developmentally appropriate chores and be consistent on follow through to ensure that they are completed. Keep offering support with chores until they become a habit.<br>5. Use external motivation, such as allowing your child to select what he is working for from a menu of reinforcements, all of which are acceptable to you. The menu items don't have to be material things but can be things like an opportunity to choose what the family is having for dinner. Samples of reinforcement charts are readily available on the Internet. |
| Doesn't seem to take pride in accomplishments | 1. Enlist your child's help in setting small goals that are within reach.<br>2. Encourage family members and friends to recognize accomplishments.<br>3. Ensure that older siblings do not belittle accomplishments.<br>4. Provide lots of opportunities for success.<br>5. Make sure your child has had opportunities to earn rewards for hard work. Karate or Taekwondo provide a leveled system and recognition. |

*Table 14, continued*

| Characteristics | Activities to Strengthen Motivation |
|---|---|
| Doesn't seem to take pleasure in any constructive activities | 1. Discuss with your pediatrician to rule out medical causes and/or a mental health therapist to rule out depression or a mental illness.<br>2. Let your child help plan a family or parent/child outing.<br>3. Have playdates planned around structured activities, like bowling, miniature golf, seeing a movie, etc.<br>4. Recognize efforts when your child participates in an activity.<br>5. Try to provide opportunities for your child to develop expertise in an area, whether it is sports, music, dance, cooking, etc. These skills provide opportunities for your child to connect with others.<br>6. Introduce the concept of living a balanced life with time for scheduled activities, physical activities, nutrition, rest, and relaxation. |

Technology, especially calendars and reminders, can be invaluable in helping your child with initiating jobs. Some useful apps and tips include:

- Remember the Milk (free): Provides easy to-do lists and reminders.
- EpicWin ($2.99): A to-do list in which the child earns points and rewards to be used to improve an avatar.
- 30/30 (free): Includes a timer to help children manage tasks and can help break larger tasks into smaller ones.
- Pomodoro Timer ($1.99): A time management app that uses a timer to break down work into intervals followed by short breaks.
- Apple's Siri has a voice-activated timer that features a time management technique involving working in blocks of time with a break.
- Microsoft Outlook can be customized to color code and list tasks according to due dates.

**Possible careers for adults with strengths or weaknesses in motivation.** Adults with strengths in motivation often move up the ladder quickly in any chosen profession in business, education, medicine, or law. Entrepreneurs are often highly motivated.

Adults who are weak in motivation might benefit from tightly controlled external motivation, like having a quota to meet in a sales job or highly structured jobs, like stocking shelves, or careers in which there are continually people to be served, such as working as clerks in stores.

**Example of someone who overcame difficulties with motivation and initiation.** Wendy Davis is a successful actress who played Colonel Joan Burton on the TV show *Army Wives* (2007–2013) for seven seasons. Davis was diagnosed with ADHD as an adult when she was already working on *Army Wives*, whereas her daughter was diagnosed as a second grader (Buningh, 2013). Figure 8 details how Davis overcame her issues with motivation in order to succeed.

## Emotional Stability and Behavioral Control

**Background information.** Hallmarks of ADHD are impulsivity and overreaction. The end results are usually behaviors and words the child would like to take back if he had been able to stop and think before letting them fly. Children blurting out rude comments to relatives or teachers, or grabbing toys from friends (or worse, hitting friends) are prime examples. These situations cause parenting to be a very humbling experience, but we have all been there. When lack of emotional stability or behavioral control occurs, don't be disheartened. Try to dissect the event and look at possible causes. Remember that all behaviors have a root cause and are reflective of your child's needs. Was your child tired . . . hungry . . . bored? Or did your child lack the skills necessary to handle the situation—like poor self-regulation skills, difficulty with delayed gratification, or inability to stop and think before reacting? If you think the cause was one of the first three, you can easily modify the schedule to manage those situations. If your child doesn't have the skills necessary to handle a situation similar to what occurred, read on for more information about enhancing those skills.

| Who | Wendy Davis, Actress |
|---|---|
| **Natural Talents** | Intrapersonal and Interpersonal |
| **Factor(s) That Needed Strengthening** | Motivation: "I struggled through primary school with Cs and the occasional D and had absolutely no ambition for my future" (p. 11). |
| **Key(s) to Success** | Davis discovered her passion for acting in her senior year of high school when she was stage manager for a production of *Annie Get Your Gun*: "I became obsessively passionate about acting and I began to excel. This was a new experience for me in an academic setting. I went from a kid who was in danger of giving up on school altogether to an honor roll student on an academic scholarship. My self-confidence began to grow. I found a profession that really utilized the creative side of my ADHD brain" (p. 11). |
| **Advice** | "Living with ADHD can be very challenging at times, and it's easy to feel sorry for yourself. Yet pity will not make the situation better. What will help you during those challenging ADHD moments is a positive attitude about yourself. . . . Fill yourself with positive energy and then choose to learn from the challenge that just knocked you off your horse. You'll be able to overcome that challenge when it comes around again because you actually took the time to figure out how to overcome it. Become an ADHD problem solver" (p. 13). |

*Figure 8.* Wendy Davis and motivation (Buningh, 2013).

Emotional stability can be influenced by many factors, including genetics, environment, and relationships. Some children seem to be born much more temperamental than others and require significantly more parental and adult support to learn how to manage their big emotions. Some families carry genetic predispositions to depression, anxiety, and other mental illnesses that can result in emotional instability. Regardless of the situation, be assured that providing a loving, secure environment with the necessary supports can make a huge difference.

The ability to stop and think before acting is a very complex mental activity. Impulse control requires:

- using nonverbal working memory to recall similar events and outcomes,
- "using self-talk or internal dialogue" to guide behavior (Forgan & Richey, 2015, p. 41), and
- shifting thinking about a situation to engage in problem solving and evaluating the outcomes of various choices.

*Some children seem to be born much more temperamental than others and require significantly more parental and adult support to learn how to manage their big emotions.*

As you know, there is a neurological and a developmental basis for impulse control. If you think back to your child's toddler years, she probably acted on impulse more times than not. Self-control starts developing at age 2 but continues through late childhood and even into adolescence for some children with ADHD. Children with ADHD are known to lag 2–3 years behind peers in the development of some skills, including impulse control. See Figure 9 for an overview of the development of impulse control. The general guidelines outlined in the figure are compiled from information from the Center on the Developing Child at Harvard University (2011), as well as research from Barkley (1997) and Teeter (1998) about what to expect at different ages.

**How weaknesses in emotional stability and behavioral control appear in children.** A child with deficits in emotional stability and behavioral control has difficulty maintaining an even disposition and/or thinking about consequences before engaging in a reaction. The child may appear very temperamental and volatile. If things don't go her way, the child may yell at others, stomp away, hit, or have a tantrum. Of course, the behavioral presentation will depend on the age. The child may appear to wear emotions on her sleeve and be easily

| | |
|---|---|
| 4–5 years | ■ "Can delay eating a treat; . . . can keep an arbitrary rule in mind and follow it to produce a response that differs from their natural instinct" (Center on the Developing Child, 2014, p. 9) |
| 6–9 years | ■ Are more internal in thinking and more adept at controlling momentary impulses |
| 10–12 years | ■ Become more flexible in thinking and able to switch between a central focus like driving and peripheral stimuli that may need attention, such as pedestrians (Center on the Developing Child, 2014) |

*Figure 9.* Guidelines for impulse control development. From *The Impulsive, Disorganized Child: Solutions for Parenting Kids With Executive Functioning Difficulties* (p. 41), by J. W. Forgan and M. A. Richey, 2015, Waco, TX: Prufrock Press. Copyright 2015 by Prufrock Press. Reprinted with permission.

angered by the opinions or actions of others, taking things more personally than intended.

To further understand children's impulse difficulties, consider what Siegel and Bryson (2018) called the *downstairs brain* and the *upstairs brain*. The downstairs brain represents the primitive parts of the brain controlling strong emotions and basic functions, like breathing and eating. Think about emotional responses in 2-year-olds. When their needs are not met, their "go-to" responses are to scream out or cry. The upstairs brain is still under construction in children and is "in charge of more complex thinking, emotional and relational skills. . . . The upstairs brain allows us to plan ahead, consider consequences, and solve difficult problems" (p. 20). As children age, we want them to use their upstairs brain, where all areas of the brain connect, rather than relying on the reactive part of their brain. Siegel and Bryson used zones (red, green, and blue) to depict children's emotional states. The goal is to keep kids in the green zone where they are able to use their upstairs brain. In the red zone, they will be reactive and act before engaging their thinking. Think of a volcano exploding. In the blue zone, children may withdraw and may appear to be immobilized.

**Strategies for strengthening emotional stability and behavioral control.** Emotional stability and behavioral control are clearly some of the most challenging aspects of ADHD. There is no one-size-fits-all approach to strengthening skills in these areas. The best thing you can do is read a variety of materials supported by research and choose the ideas that you feel will work with your family structure and personalities involved. Remember that children's behaviors respond to a variety of techniques and styles as long as there is consistency in the structure, love, and basic needs are met. The purpose of our book is to empower you to do the best you can for your child, not cause you to mentally beat yourself up because you do not feel you are succeeding with your child. In our experience, all parents feel that way at one time or another. The fact that you are reading this book speaks to your desire to help your child. Move forward knowing that some of our suggestions will work with your child and others won't. As parents of successful, well-adjusted, and happy adult children, we can tell you that the results are worth every ounce of effort you put into the important job of rearing your child. Table 15 is a list of strategies for strengthening emotional stability and behavioral control in your child.

**Resources for strengthening emotional stability and behavioral control.** Books for children include:

- *My Mouth Is a Volcano!* by Julia Cook (age 4 and older)
- *Mindful Monkey, Happy Panda* by Lauren Alderfer (ages 4–8)
- *Sitting Still Like a Frog: Mindfulness Exercises for Kids* by Eline Snel (ages 5–12)
- *How Do You Doodle? Drawing My Feelings and Emotions* by Elise Gravel (ages 6–10)
- *Take The Time: Mindfulness for Kids* by Maud Roegiers (age 6 and older)
- *Learning to Feel Good and Stay Cool: Emotional Regulation Tools for Kids With AD/HD* by Judith Glasser and Kathleen G. Nadeau (ages 9–12)
- *Understanding Myself: A Kid's Guide to Intense Emotions and Strong Feelings* by Mary C. Lamia (ages 8–13)

*Table 15*
Strategies for Strengthening Emotional Stability and Behavioral Control

| Characteristics | Activities to Strengthen Emotional Stability and Behavioral Control |
| --- | --- |
| Doesn't maintain an even disposition | 1. When your child is out of control, don't try to reason with her until she has returned to equilibrium.<br>2. Help her label what she is experiencing. Is it boredom, anger, worry, discomfort, frustration, etc.?<br>3. Encourage maintaining a big-picture view by asking questions like, "Next week, do you think you will remember this incident?"<br>4. Provide your child help in recognizing signs that mood is shifting and work with her to identify possible interventions. |
| Has limited self-control | 1. Try to help your child understand that ADHD often makes it more difficult to practice self-control, but it is something you can work on together.<br>2. Identify triggers and circumstances in which loss of self-control happens most often, and try to engineer the environment for success and provide additional support when needed.<br>3. Provide visuals when possible. For example, if a child is blurting out in class, have a laminated picture of him raising his hand. If he often needs the teacher's help, provide two color-coded cards—one indicating he can continue working until the teacher can get to him and another indicating he is totally stuck and doesn't know what to do next. At the same time, encourage independence in finding his solutions.<br>4. Practice learning to stop and think about long-term consequences before acting.<br>5. Encourage your child to remove himself from the situation until self-control returns—like a self-imposed timeout.<br>6. Use communication skills to talk through a situation—either with the others involved or through self-talk that can be internal. |

*Table 15, continued*

| Characteristics | Activities to Strengthen Emotional Stability and Behavioral Control |
|---|---|
| Does not utilize coping strategies | 1. Develop a list of strategies that work for your child, such as taking deep breaths, using self-talk, calling on past experiences, or visualizing herself in a calm place. (See the coping menu in Appendix B.)<br>2. Provide opportunities to observe others in the environment and identify coping strategies other children use.<br>3. Use literature to learn how others employ coping strategies.<br>4. Make sure adults in the child's environment are modeling appropriate coping strategies. |
| Doesn't think before acting | 1. Try to anticipate situations in which impulsive behavior occurs so you can be prepared to cue the child to stop and think.<br>2. Encourage stop-and-think strategies in your child, such as taking a deep breath, counting to 3, or visualizing a stop sign in front of his face before acting to provide time to think about the consequences of the action and possibly better alternatives.<br>3. Role-play different scenarios with your child, such as when someone grabs a toy or when he is excluded on the playground, so he has practice in handling different kinds of situations. |

- *Chillax! How Ernie Learns to Chill Out, Relax, and Take Charge of His Anger* by Marcella Marino Craver (ages 8–13)
- *Emotions! Making Sense of Your Feelings* by Mary Lamia (ages 15–18)

Games for children include:
- I Feel Angry When . . . teaches children to communicate using I-messages and includes 12 anger control strategies (ages 6–12): https://www.creativetherapystore.com/products/i-feel-angry-when
- Angry Animals 2 teaches healthy expression of anger by having players pick appropriate responses for a given scenario

(ages 5–10): https://www.creativetherapystore.com/products/angry-animals-2
- Emotional ABCs Help your Child Succeed: Features workbooks with activities, playing cards designed to teach basic emotional skills, and a DVD for children to help them understand their emotions (ages 4 and up): https://www.emotionalabcs.com

Books for adults include:
- *The Yes Brain Child: How to Cultivate Courage, Curiosity, and Resilience in Your Child* by Daniel J. Siegel and Tina Payne Bryson
- *The Impulsive, Disorganized Child: Solutions for Parenting Kids With Executive Functioning Difficulties* by James W. Forgan and Mary Anne Richey
- *The Explosive Child: A New Approach for Understanding and Parenting Easily Frustrated, Chronically Inflexible Children* by Ross W. Greene
- *Your Defiant Child: Eight Steps to Better Behavior* by Russell Barkley and Christine Benton
- *Smart But Stuck: Emotions in Teens and Adults With ADHD* by Thomas E. Brown

Some useful online resources and apps include:
- Video: "Social Skills Video: Taking a Break to Calm Down" (available at https://www.youtube.com/watch?v=YMM67Le2VHA)
- Daniel Tiger's Grr-ific Feelings ($2.99): Helps young children identify and express emotions through games and songs.
- Smiling Mind (free): Provides mindfulness activities, including breathing exercises and listening to music.
- Breathe, Think, Do With Sesame (free): Teaches young children to breath, think, and then do.
- Stop, Breathe & Think (free): A meditation app for middle schoolers and older teens.

**Possible careers for adults with strengths or weaknesses in emotional stability and/or behavioral control.** Adults with strengths in emotional stability and behavioral control stay in command of their emotions, even in crises, and are able to act responsibly and are often successful as policemen, emergency room medical personnel, teachers and principals, event planners, plumbers, and facility managers—any kind of career that requires people to think on their feet.

Adults with weaknesses in these areas would likely do better in fields that do not require them to interact with others in any problem-solving capacity and that would offer some opportunities to use coping mechanisms like stepping away from a problem for a few minutes to regroup. Jobs that are routine and more solitary, such as accounting, house cleaning, or home maintenance, like painting or landscaping, might be good career choices.

**Example of someone who overcame difficulties with emotional stability and behavioral control.** Linda Pinney is a successful entrepreneur. She is the founder and chief business officer of Asteres, a company enabling prescription drugs to be dispensed by machine. Her latest endeavor is The Startup Lab, a company serving venture capital firms. Pinney was diagnosed with ADHD well into adulthood while seeing a therapist for other issues (Corman & Hallowell, 2006). Figure 10 details how Pinney overcame her issues with behavioral control in order to succeed.

## Integrity

**Background information.** Honesty and behavior consistent with one's moral code are considered to be the hallmarks of integrity. A person with integrity can be counted on to do the right thing, regardless of the circumstances—sometimes a rare commodity. Integrity has been described as "a wholeness of character that includes what's good for both self and others" (Chandler, 2001, p. 38). Integrity is often influenced by environment and role models, but not always. We have seen very honest parents dumbfounded at the dishonesty of their children.

| Who | Linda Pinney, Entrepreneur |
|---|---|
| **Natural Talents** | Logical, Visual-Spatial, and Bodily-Kinesthetic |
| **Factor(s) That Needed Strengthening** | Behavioral Control: Pinney was a permanent fixture in the principal's office in elementary school. Her behavioral troubles continued into high school despite her parents' efforts to redirect her boundless energy into competitive sports and chores. She said that her parents and teachers couldn't understand that she didn't intentionally cause so much trouble. In high school, "Linda collected more pink slips than any other student in the history of her high school. . . . Linda was oblivious to the effects her actions had on others. She could never figure out, for instance, how she managed to reduce teachers to tears" (p. 141). <br><br> Organization: Pinney's difficulty with organizational skills caused her problems and followed her to college. "Still plagued by disorganization, Linda would sometimes sit in on the wrong class or show up at the wrong place to take exams" (p. 143). |
| **Key(s) to Success** | Pinney's parents recognized very early that she needed multiple outlets for her boundless energy and signed her up for sports of all types. She excelled at individuals sports more than team sports, partially because of her difficulty with understanding other people. Her parents also provided a structured environment and gave her lots of chores to keep her busy, like caring for the family pets, helping with the laundry and doing yard work. Additionally, her high school was able to see her strengths as well as her difficulties. At an awards ceremony her senior year of high school, she was awarded a leadership award. In college, she benefitted from being able to study areas that interested her. She ultimately earned two master's degrees—one in business and the other in health care. She tired of her relationship difficulties and sought the help of a therapist as an adult. The therapist recognized her ADHD and sent her to a psychiatrist, who prescribed medication that helped with her impulsivity. |
| **Advice** | "Her advice to kids is that even though much of what they have to say is right, they have to think about when they say it" (p. 147). She stressed the importance of understanding how important timing is in what people say and do. |

*Figure 10.* Linda Pinney and behavioral control (Corman & Hallowell, 2006).

Many complex constructs are at work in integrity, including:
- empathy, or understanding how another person is feeling;
- strength of character or staying the course, regardless of the circumstances;
- morals;
- an internal compass, informing the child about right and wrong; and
- thinking beyond immediate gratification or selfish needs.

**How weaknesses in integrity appear in children.** A child who has difficulty with integrity doesn't accept responsibility for wrongdoing, has difficulty keeping commitments and respecting others, and is dishonest. The child may bully others, lie to people, refuse to apologize for any wrongdoing, or may cheat or steal. Lying can be particularly troubling in children, especially if it becomes habitual. Children with ADHD often have difficulty with lying for a variety of reasons, which can include disbelief that they have actually committed the act when that wasn't their intention, lack of recall of the action, or an attempt to save face following repeated failures. If your child is lying, it is important to try to figure out what is behind it. Figure 11 discusses several different scenarios that can occur with children with ADHD.

**Strategies for strengthening integrity.** Regardless of the cause, it is important to address integrity and lying in such a manner that the child knows that lying or lack of integrity is not acceptable in your family. As a child, Mary Anne remembers her parents saying that there was no situation that would be made worse by telling the truth about it. When a child has lied, it is important for him to own up to the lie and figure out how to make amends. Talk through the situation to determine solutions that would have worked better and have enabled your child to come away with his integrity intact. Help your child understand that lying impacts others in a negative way as well. Remember that if your child has been using lying as a coping skill, it will take patience, consistency, and time to change it. Table 16 is a list of strategies for strengthening integrity skills in your child.

| Scenario | What Could Be at Play |
|---|---|
| You ask your teenager to start the washing machine and she doesn't, claiming you never told her to do it. | Forgetfulness and poor listening skills: Perhaps she is not lying and really didn't remember your request. |
| Your child steals a small toy from her best friend and is very vocal in denying she took it. | Impulsivity in speaking before thinking through the situation: She may be surprised that she couldn't control her own impulses. |
| Your child claims he did his homework when he didn't. | Embarrassment at not knowing how to do it: He may be attempting to avoid an unpleasant task or be unable to think ahead to consequences. |
| Your child has been taking gymnastics for years in anticipation of being a cheerleader. He told you he was attending cheerleading tryouts but didn't. | Anxiety: He may fear shame and rejection. |

*Figure 11.* Potential scenarios in which children with ADHD may be or appear to be lying.

**Resources for strengthening integrity.** Books for children include:

- *The Berenstain Bears and the Truth* by Stan and Jan Berenstain (ages 3–7)
- *David Gets in Trouble* by David Shannon (ages 4–8)
- *The Boy Who Cried Bigfoot* by Scott Magoon (ages 4–8)
- *Eli's Lie-O-Meter: A Story about Telling the Truth* by Sandra Levins (ages 4–8)
- *Pinky Promise: A Book About Telling the Truth* by Vanita Braver (ages 5–6)
- *The Empty Pot* by Demi (ages 5–8)
- *Telling the Truth: Learning About Honesty, Integrity, and Trustworthiness* by Regina Burch (ages 5–8)
- *The Stories Julian Tells* by Ann Cameron (ages 6–9)
- *Liar, Liar* by Gary Paulsen (ages 8–12)

*Table 16*
Strategies to Strengthen Your Child's Integrity

| Characteristics | Activities to Strengthen Integrity |
|---|---|
| Is dishonest | 1. Be a good role model in being honest in daily interactions and talking to your child about it.<br>2. Make it a family value.<br>3. Praise honesty when it is displayed, but confront dishonesty openly but respectfully.<br>4. Create a relationship in which a child will be able to own up to a lie.<br>5. Have consequences for lying.<br>6. When disciplining your child, consider showing some grace if your child is honest about the wrongdoing. |
| Doesn't respect others | 1. Play games with opportunities for winning and losing.<br>2. Help develop empathy and understanding of how actions impact others' feelings.<br>3. Assist in engaging in volunteer activities that help develop awareness of other people's situations.<br>4. Encourage your child to become part of a church group or Boy or Girl Scouts where mutual respect is a core value. |
| Doesn't take responsibility for actions | 1. Help with practicing accepting compliments and criticism.<br>2. Role-play situations with positive and negative outcomes, such as when a friendship was saved when someone apologized or a plan was made to finish chores that were forgotten.<br>3. Talk to your child about experiences in his own life in which children have not accepted responsibility for their actions, like if a playmate broke a toy or hurt someone's feelings. |
| Doesn't keep commitments | 1. Help your child understand how others are impacted through discussion, role-playing, and stories.<br>2. Make sure that your child does not have a problem with organization or keeping a calendar. If so, see the section in this chapter on organization.<br>3. If your child commits to an activity or sports team, make sure she completes the season.<br>4. Help your child understand the value of keeping his word, such as the saying, "Your word is your bond."<br>5. Make sure you keep your commitments to your child. |

Games for children include:
- Building Character: Play-2-Learn Dominoes is a dominoes game for 2–5 players that teaches respect, honesty, fairness, caring, and responsibility (grades 1–5): https://www.childtherapy toys.com/products/building-character-play-2-learn-dominoes
- Who's Responsible? The Game That Teaches Kids to do the Right Thing . . . Even When Nobody's Looking is much like the classic detective game Clue (ages 7–12): https://www.childtherapytoys.com/products/whos-responsible-game
- Scruples is a game of moral dilemmas: https://scruplesgame.com
- Parents.com's "Good Behavior Games for Preschoolers" are simple games that involve everyday items from around the house: https://www.parents.com/toddlers-preschoolers/development/manners/good-behavior-games-for-preschoolers

Books for adults include:
- *10-Minute Life Lessons for Kids: 52 Fun and Simple Games and Activities to Teach Your Child Honesty, Trust, Love, and Other Important Values* by Jamie Miller
- *How Children Succeed: Grit, Curiosity, and the Hidden Power of Character* by Paul Tough

**Possible careers for adults with strengths or weaknesses in integrity.** Adults with strengths in integrity are dependable, honest, and respectful of others and may be policemen, judges, medical ethicists, public service officials, or teachers. Businesses that offer dependable and honest services are always in demand.

Adults with weaknesses in integrity will likely have difficulty in any job but might do better in areas in which there are strict controls, few temptations in handling money or material goods, and few opportunities to use their own judgment, such as working on street crews, pursuing manual labor jobs, or being part of an assembly line in a factory.

**Example of someone who overcame difficulties with integrity.** Norman is a successful electrician who is about to start his own company. He was diagnosed with ADHD at 5 years old. Figure 12 details how Norman overcame his issues with integrity in order to succeed.

## Social Skills

**Background information.** Many of us take social skills for granted, but they involve neurodevelopmental functions that are quite complicated. They involve personality characteristics as well as specific skills, such as:

- desire for social interaction,
- receptive (processing and understanding language) and expressive language,
- the ability to stop and observe body language and conversations before speaking,
- working memory to recall and draw on any similar situations,
- the ability to organize thoughts and decide on a response,
- adequate eye contact, and
- appropriate body language.

Levine (2002) divided the process of being social into two categories: (1) social language, which entails oral communication appropriate for the situation; and (2) social behaviors, which include regulating outward behavior like dressing appropriately for the situation, not standing too close to a person, and showing proper facial expressions. Levine noted that social difficulties can be the result of struggles in one or both areas. In our practices, we have seen children who are able to verbally communicate with other children but annoy them because they invade people's personal space by standing too close, look away when talking rather than making eye contact, or fail to do their part when getting ready for an event. On the other hand, we have seen children who always behave appropriately by doing their part of groupwork, have proper facial expressions to match a situation, dress appropriately, and respect others' personal space, but they can't com-

| Who | Norman, Electrician |
| --- | --- |
| **Natural Talents** | Visual-spatial and Kinesthetic |
| **Factor(s) That Needed Strengthening** | Integrity and grit: Norman was the youngest of five children in a family in which success was expected. School was always a big struggle for him. He stumbled along with C's and D's, much less successful than his academically inclined older brothers and sisters. He began medication at age 8, but that did not seem to help his academic problems. He felt his parents were constantly pressuring him about school and homework, so he resorted to lying, cheating on tests, and making excuses for his poor performance. He knew college wasn't for him and drifted from one menial job to another, barely making enough money to live on his own. He had a chance for a sales job selling electrical supplies with good pay, but it required a college degree. He had a friend help him fill out the application and lied about going to college, even listing a degree. He nailed the interview and was sure he could do the job. A background check revealed he had falsified the application. His interviewer had been impressed with his knowledge of electrical systems and called him back in to discuss the inaccuracy. Norman disclosed his struggles with ADHD while in school. The interviewer convinced Norman that he had recognizable strengths and didn't need to lie about his credentials. He suggested that he work with an ADHD coach to get a better handle on his life, so that he could use the strengths he had. |
| **Key(s) to Success** | Norman learned to accept his ADHD diagnosis and try not to run from it. He felt years of failure had driven him to lying because he couldn't figure out how to manage otherwise. Seeing an ADHD coach helped him come to terms with his strengths and weaknesses and how to avoid jobs that did not play to his strengths. |
| **Advice** | "If you are struggling in school, try to find a teacher who can help you understand your problems and work with you to make things better. My parents didn't understand my ADHD, but I feel like I could have found someone at my school who would have. Lying to cover up is only a temporary fix and just makes things worse in the end." |

*Figure 12.* Norman and integrity.

municate what they are thinking or carry their part of a conversation. Deficits in either area, social language or social behavior, can cause angst and unhappiness for your child.

Some of the social language signposts that Levine (2002) advised parents to be aware of include:

- communication and interpretation of feelings,
- matching communication style to fit the people present,
- selecting appropriate topics of conversation and staying on the topic,
- using the correct tone of voice for the situation,
- knowing how to ask for something without alienating people,
- being able to take the perspective of the other person,
- understanding the mood and matching it to language (e.g., not laughing when it is a serious conversation or realizing when someone is telling a joke), and
- complimenting (p. 232).

Levine (2002) categorized important social behaviors as follows:

- being able to resolve conflicts with others without aggression,
- monitoring interaction to judge how it is going and whether it is appropriate,
- collaborating and working with others as a team,
- interpreting social incidences (especially people's reactions), and
- maintaining a good public image (p. 237).

These social language and social behavior skills are developmental. During the early preschool years, children are often very egocentric, concerned mainly about what they want, and engage in lots of parallel play. As they prepare to enter elementary school, they start to be more aware of the needs of others, benefit from collaboration, and can share experiences and possessions. By second or third grade, children start to be aware of popularity and often become less accepting of others. Cliques develop, and bullying may begin by third grade.

# Keys to Success

No matter how socially competent your child is, you will probably live through a series of social ups and downs. Your child may be best friends with someone one day and ignored the following day. Such is the way of elementary friendships in which kids are learning to navigate complex social networks. Try to be a good sounding board. Don't minimize hurt feelings but validate them, saying things like, "That must have really hurt your feelings," or "That must have really surprised you." Sometimes by talking through a situation with a trusted adult, a child will determine his own way forward. Try to assess your child's social strengths and weaknesses and provide support when needed.

Also keep in mind that girls and boys often differ in how they develop friendships. Boys' friendships often develop around activities in which there are shared interests, such as playing basketball, fishing, or playing video games. Girls, on the other hand, tend to seek out other girls with whom they can share conversation and inner thoughts, as well as give and receive mutual support. These differences continue into adulthood, in which men often get together for a golf or bowling game, whereas often women go to lunch so they can share conversation.

Children with adequate social skills are generally much happier and lead more satisfying lives than those who struggle with relationships. Any parent who has felt the sting of their child not being invited to birthday parties knows that the pain of exclusion is very real. We have all seen children who give up trying to make friends and become reclusive, which is very different from the introvert who likes to spend some time alone. Video games and the extensive use of devices and smartphones make it easy for older children and teens to become lost in a virtual world rather than engaging socially. Strong social skills are important for today's children in many settings, including among peers and on social media and the Internet. Issues can arise in several areas:

- **Peer pressure:** Peer pressure is a critical issue to be dealt with in later elementary school and especially in middle and high school. Social skills can give your child confidence to remain true to her values, rather than being coerced into following the crowd and becoming preoccupied with popularity. Researchers in New Zealand followed more than 1,000 children over a 9-year period and concluded that children "who have problematic peer relationships at age nine tend to have significantly less success in school and employment than those who get along reasonably well with their peers during childhood." (Brown, 2014, p. 94). The children who were least successful socially at age 9 were also five times more likely to become unemployed after leaving school.

- **Social media and cyberbullying:** Social media significantly changed how people interact. We have probably all seen gatherings of kids in which no one is talking to each other; they are all texting or using an app on their phones. Often conversations are in short, incomplete sentences with little in-depth, verbal communication occurring. Your child's social environment will continue to change as technology advances. The accessibility of information can be positive, but there are also pitfalls. Social issues have taken on a whole different level of complexity with the advent of social media. Children are using social media at younger and younger ages. Older children in elementary school may be exposed to cyberbullying— mean, threatening, or demeaning messages delivered over the Internet. Obviously, being publicly shamed is a huge source of stress and one that children may be very reluctant to disclose to others out of embarrassment, fear of retaliation, or guilt. If you do find out your child has been exposed to cyberbullying, it is important to try to see this type of harassment from a child's viewpoint. Children can't put it into perspective like adults and have difficulty projecting what their life will be like 10 years from now. Every day in the life of a child can seem like an eternity and result in a frequent refrain of "My life is ruined."
- **Online privacy:** How much privacy you allow your child on the Internet is a personal decision. A child's judgment is still a

work in progress. Based on our experience and the situations we have seen children get themselves into, we advise supervision and oversight—postponing use of social media until you feel your child can exercise sound judgment, looking at what your kids are posting, knowing who their friends are, and checking on which websites they visit. Children's impulsivity may not be fully reigned in or they may not be perceptive enough to see through some Internet "come ons" or read between the lines in some conversations. Many parents have to work so hard to provide for their families that they have little energy to oversee their children's friendships and use of social media. Even when parents try to be involved, their children are often so much more sophisticated in their use of technology that they can outwit their parents. However, this is one area you cannot ignore. The government website https://www.stopbullying.gov is an excellent resource for parents.

- **Connections to nefarious groups:** Sulkowski and Picciolini (2018) reported that studies into the radicalization of youth have shown that teens who are demoralized and lack a cultural or community identity may be easy targets for extremist groups trying to lure new members. These groups try to foster the social connections that are often missing in the young person's life while introducing their extremist ideologies.

**How weaknesses in social skills appear in children.** A child with deficits in this area often appears awkward in social situations, especially ones that are unfamiliar; may avoid eye contact; has little or too much to say; or may interrupt. He may make conversation that doesn't fit the situation or be unable to express emotions appropriately, such as exploding over a situation rather than using language to identify and express frustration.

Social interactions are often complicated for people with ADHD because of their impulsivity and difficulty with other executive functions. They often have trouble stopping long enough to think of the impact of what they say or do before blurting something out. Often, they don't stay focused on an interaction long enough to determine what is really going on or may miss important social cues. If they have difficulty with working memory, they may interrupt conversations to say what they want to say because they are afraid they will forget if they wait. If they have difficulty with organizational skills, they may intend to show up to help with a group project or keep a commitment but lose track of time and miss the engagement.

**Strategies for strengthening social skills.** A child's social prowess is based on genetics, personality, social experiences, role models, language development, emotional control, and sometimes even physical appearance. If one of your child's strength areas from the Keys to Success Survey was intrapersonal intelligence, your child may need time alone to process thoughts, make plans, and just "be." You don't want to try to change your child from an introvert to an extrovert because that would go against his or her nature. Many introverts have friendships; they just don't feel the need to engage with others as much as extroverts do. An introvert with strong social skills understands when to be a support person and when to be a leader, and has the flexibility to be either as the situation demands. The important thing is to assess whether or not your quiet child has the skills and the self-confidence to use them when needed.

We have seen children who are considered to be "loners" just because they don't have the social skills required. If that is the case, you definitely want to work to try to equip your child with abilities to handle herself in many different situations or get professional help if need be. Many speech/language pathologists provide language therapy for social language, called pragmatics, and some counselors and therapists offer social skills groups. Social relationships can be a very important buffer against some of the harsh realities of life and important for a successful adult life, so it is important for your child to have at least one or two good friends. These friends can provide a sense of security and belonging.

Table 17 is a list of further strategies for strengthening your child's social skills.

*Table 17*

Strategies to Strengthen Your Child's Social Skills

| Characteristics | Activities to Strengthen Social Skills |
|---|---|
| Has difficulty maintaining friendships | 1. Have structured playdates centered around specific activities, such as bowling, swimming, or playing in the park.<br>2. Observe if your child is missing critical skills, like sharing belongings, keeping a conversation going, expressing emotions appropriately, or respecting the other person. Practice role-playing different scenarios to help reinforce the missing skills.<br>3. Enlist the teacher's help in figuring out why your child might be having trouble. Ask for any suggestions on children who might make a good friend for your child.<br>4. Talk with your child about lunch and recess to find out if he is playing with or talking to anyone. Help him brainstorm topics to talk about and games to play at recess. |
| Is uncooperative in group efforts | Younger children:<br>1. Play games in which your child has to take turns playing different roles and help him see how all are important.<br>2. Practice turn-taking in conversation.<br>3. Role-play situations in which you and your child take turns being the leader and the participant.<br><br>Older children:<br>1. Talk with your child about situations in your own life in which you have benefitted from taking on different roles in a group.<br>2. Try to understand why your child has a hard time cooperating: Does she feel disrespected, want only to be the leader, or know how to communicate her displeasure with the direction of the group?<br>3. Help your child understand something about group dynamics and especially how to communicate respectfully in a group situation. |
| Doesn't identify or express feelings appropriately | 1. Use feelings wheels or visual charts to help your child learn to identify feelings.<br>2. When your child does express a feeling to you, such as sadness, don't minimize it. Instead, help your child learn that feelings are acceptable. It is how the feelings are handled that makes the difference. |

*Table 17, continued*

| Characteristics | Activities to Strengthen Social Skills |
|---|---|
| Younger children: Doesn't respect personal space, gets too close to others<br><br>Older children: Is slow to pick up social clues | **Younger children:**<br>1. Teach personal boundaries by allowing your child to have some private space of her own. Have a closed-door policy when changing clothes or using the bathroom.<br>2. Teach the concept of personal space by having your child put his arms out straight and look around. That is a good example of how much space should be between him and another when talking.<br>3. Have your child step inside a hula hoop for another example of personal space.<br>4. Establish a special cue, such as touching her arm when she is standing too close to someone.<br><br>**Older children:**<br>1. Watch a TV show and discuss the characters' facial expressions, tone of voice, and body language.<br>2. Read stories aloud with dialogue and practice different intonations.<br>3. Have your child practice reading facial expressions of family members and guess the feeling behind the expressions. |

**Resources for strengthening social skills.** Books for children include:

- *It's Mine!* by Leo Lionni (ages 3–7)
- *Peanut Butter and Jellyous . . . Sometimes Friendships Get Sticky* by Michael Genhart (ages 4–8)
- *Mac and Geeeez! . . . Being Real Is What It's All About* by Michael Genhart (ages 4–8)
- *Cake and I Scream! . . . Being Bossy Isn't Sweet* by Michael Genhart (ages 4–8)
- *Dealing With Bullies* by Pam Scheunemann (ages 4–6)
- *The Juice Box Bully: Empowering Kids to Stand Up for Others* by Bob Sornson and Maria Dismondy (ages 4 and up)
- *Martha Doesn't Share!* by Samantha Berger (ages 4 and up)
- *Chrysanthemum* by Kevin Henkes (ages 4–8)
- *Big Red and the Little Bitty Wolf: A Story About Bullying* by Jeanie Franz Ransom (ages 4–8)

# Keys to Success

- *Blossom Plays Possum (Because She's Shy)* by Birdy Jones (ages 4–8)
- *Sally Sore Loser: A Story About Winning and Losing* by Frank J. Sileo (ages 4–8)
- *I Don't Know Why . . . I Guess I'm Shy: A Story About Taming Imaginary Fears* by Barbara S. Cain (ages 4–8)
- *Boss No More* by Estelle Meens (ages 4–8)
- *There's a Cat in Our Class!: A Tale About Getting Along* by Jeanie Franz Ransom (ages 4–8)
- *Toodles and Teeny: A Story About Friendship* by Jill Neimark and Marcella Bakur Weiner (ages 4–8)
- *Friends Always* by Tanja Wenisch (ages 4–8)
- *I'm Like You, You're Like Me: A Child's Book About Understanding and Appreciating Each Other* by Cindy Gainer (ages 4–8)
- *Ouch Moments: When Words Are Used in Hurtful Ways* by Michael Genhart (ages 6–8)
- Positive Steps series: *Respecting Others, Caring for Others,* and *Respecting Others* by Susan Martineau (ages 6–10)
- *Blue Cheese Breath and Stinky Feet: How to Deal With Bullies* by Catherine DePino (ages 6–12)
- *Stand Up for Yourself and Your Friends: Dealing With Bullies and Bossiness and Finding a Better Way* by Patti Kelley Criswell (girls, ages 8 and up)
- *Circle of Three: Enough Friendship to Go Around?* by Elizabeth Brokamp (ages 8–12)
- *Learning to Be Kind and Understand Differences: Empathy Skills For Kids With AD/HD* by Judith Glasser and Jill Menkes Kushner (ages 8–12)

Games for children include:
- Blunders by Aimee Symington (ages 5–10) teaches children about social and dining etiquette.
- How to Be a Bully! NOT! by Marcia Nass is a book and card game for young children that teaches what bullies do and how not to respond.

- You are a Social Detective! by Michelle Garcia Winner and Pamela Crooke (grades K–5)

Books for adults include *Nobody Likes Me, Everybody Hates Me: The Top 25 Friendship Problems and How to Solve Them* by Michele Borba.

Some useful online resources include:

- "4 Social Situations to Role-Play With Your Grade-Schooler" by Lexi Walters Wright (available at https://www.understood.org/en/friends-feelings/common-challenges/following-social-rules/4-social-situations-to-role-play-with-your-child): Features several social situations to role-play with your child.
- Social Thinking: Free Articles & Strategies (available at https://www.socialthinking.com/Resources): Michelle Garcia Winner is one of the leaders in the field of social skills, especially for children with autism, but she also has information about children with ADHD. Free articles are available on her website. She also has webinars, which are fee-based.
- "16 YouTube Videos That Teach Social Skills" by ADDitude Editors and Anna Vagin (available at https://www.additudemag.com/slideshows/youtube-videos-for-kids): A collection of valuable videos for kids.

**Possible careers for adults with strengths or weaknesses in social skills.** People with strengths in social skills are often charismatic and expert communicators. They know how to be team players, settle disputes, and establish working relationships. They are usually happy in fields requiring frequent interaction with others and working in a team. Careers in education, social work, psychology, law, or human resources might be satisfying to these adults.

Adults with weaknesses in social skills would do better in jobs that are solitary and require little interaction with others, such as researchers, writers, mathematicians, some types of engineering, and production, such as sewing or assembly work.

**Example of someone who overcame difficulties with social skills.** Jay Carter is an ADHD coach who runs Hyperfocused Coaching Systems, LLC. He was diagnosed with ADHD as an adult while researching his daughter's learning difficulties (Brenis, 2011). Figure 13 details how Carter strengthened his social skills in order to succeed.

## Grit

**Background information.** When we think about the term *grit* and your child with ADHD, we think about encouraging her to be conscientious and persevere—even when the going gets tough. All adults know life is filled with challenges, and getting through those can often mean the difference between success and failure. Grit involves being persistent, following through on commitments, and delaying gratification for the accomplishment of an immediate goal. Delaying gratification is a difficult concept for anyone, especially children with ADHD whose reward center is more in tune to immediate gratification.

Duckworth (2016) has done extensive research on people who have gained excellence in their fields through their work ethic. She found that a combination of passion and perseverance, which she termed *grit*, is responsible for the success of those she studied. She stressed that passion and perseverance develop over time; so be patient, parents. Inherent in her concept of grit is conscientiousness. Duckworth clarified that grit isn't just talent or luck, but is instead having a goal that you continue to work toward over time. Although she studied world-class athletes, Spelling Bee champions, and musicians at the top of their fields, we can take away some important concepts from her research and theory of grit. Duckworth posed that pursuing a passion in a purposeful, practiced way can help a child develop grit, which can then be applied to other areas of life.

*Grit involves being persistent, following through on commitments, and delaying gratification for the accomplishment of an immediate goal.*

| Who | Jay Carter, ADHD coach |
|---|---|
| **Natural Talents** | Intrapersonal |
| **Factor(s) That Needed Strengthening** | Social skills: As a child, Jay was labeled a troublemaker, but that was never his intent. He said he could never understand how he had gotten in a fight or caused trouble. As an adult he realized, "It's poor social skills rather than poor productivity that often holds people with ADHD back. . . . Most people don't realize what that means in a work situation. I was never comfortable with classic networking, I wasn't really good at communicating. I didn't communicate what I was doing so people didn't realize the contribution I was making" (para. 3, para. 16). |
| **Key(s) to Success** | Jay found that he did much better when he was busy. He struggled in elementary and secondary school, and was kicked out of a boarding school. He spent a year in rehab: "If you understand ADHD, there's a lot of self-medicating related to the ADHD and the baggage you pick up living a life that's out of control" (para. 6). He married someone who helped provide stability and went back to school while working full time, noting that staying busy helped focus his attention. After his diagnosis, he began taking medication and switched to a job that was a better fit. He also attended ADHD support group meetings and worked with an ADHD coach. He now uses speech-recognition and mind-mapping software as well as a virtual assistant. |
| **Advice** | Jay advocates developing a good understanding of ADHD and how it impacts a person's life. In his own life, working with a coach helped him change many of his negative beliefs about himself that he had picked up over the years: "I wouldn't trade my ADHD for anything. . . There really is an aspect of giftedness to it, and if I can focus 99 percent on my strengths and keep my weaknesses from tripping me up, that's great" (para. 19). |

*Figure 13.* Jay Carter and social skills (Brenis, 2011).

In her effort to learn more about grit, Duckworth questioned "whether grit is not just about *quantity* of time devoted to interests, but also *quality* of time. Not just *more time on task*, but also *better time on task*" (p. 118). She reviewed the research of Anders Ericsson, a professor of psychology at Florida State University, who has studied people who are top in their fields. He coined the term *deliberate practice*, which is focused, effortful practice in which the person is "working where challenges exceed skill" (as cited in Duckworth, 2016, p. 129). Critical to the whole process in Duckworth's and Ericsson's models are breaking a skill down into small sub-skills to practice, engaging in focused practice, and then getting feedback about performance to ensure the sub-skills are being practiced correctly. Then that feedback is used to determine what can be done better to hasten the development of the skill.

Duckworth (2018) also developed Character Lab (https://www.characterlab.org), which is a program that uses psychological research targeted to help middle and high school students improve character strengths in the following areas: self-control, grit, curiosity, growth mindset, gratitude, purpose, social intelligence, and zest. Her program can be implemented by parents, coaches, or teachers in the classroom. She includes clear explanations of each concept and activities for development, including action steps and criteria for success.

**How weaknesses in grit appear in children.** Children with deficits in this area give up easily when faced with obstacles and can't be counted on to follow through with commitments. A child with deficits in conscientiousness often can't break a large task down into small, manageable goals. She is easily overwhelmed by obstacles and may give up quickly. For example, if reading is difficult, the child may be very reluctant to practice and work on improving his or her skills.

**Strategies for strengthening grit.** A classic example of someone with grit is Michael Phelps, whom we have mentioned previously. He retired from Olympic swimming with 28 medals (23 of which were gold medals). He became so passionate about swimming that he exercised vigorously, modified his diet, was purposeful when practicing, and would wait for hours for his turn to compete. Phelps had struggles with substance abuse, sought assistance in rehab, and returned to the pool to compete in the Olympics in 2016. Although few of us, your children included, will become the best in our fields, we can all benefit from the concept of focused practice. So many of the children we see "go through the motions" of sitting with a book and look as if they are reading for understanding, but their minds can be 1,000 miles away. To help them develop grit and perseverance, we want to praise the effort they are putting in and want to encourage quality time, not just quantity of time, on task working toward a goal.

Kara, an 8-year-old client, absolutely hated swimming because she didn't want to get her head wet. Her parents told her that learning to swim was nonnegotiable, especially living in South Florida, where water is everywhere. They found a very positive teacher who was skillful in helping children overcome their fear of water. This teacher made sure to break the skill down into small steps and provided lots of praise when each small step was accomplished. Much to Kara's surprise, she loved swimming after she became good at it and is now an avid member of a local swim team. Although she is far from being the best one on the team, she loves it. Like Kara, children may not even be good at what interests them, but become better and better over time with practice. Don't discourage your child, and give her lots of leeway in exploring interests.

Table 18 is a list of additional strategies for strengthening your child's grit.

**Resources for strengthening grit.** Books for children include:
- *Stickley Sticks to It!* by Brenda S. Miles (ages 4–8)
- *The Empty Pot* by Demi (ages 5–8)
- *Nothing You Can't Do!: The Secret Power of Growth Mindsets* by Mary Cay Ricci (ages 9–12)

Books for adults include:
- *How Children Succeed: Grit, Curiosity, and the Hidden Power of Character* by Paul Tough

# Keys to Success

*Table 18*
Strategies for Strengthening Your Child's Grit

| Characteristics | Activities to Strengthen Grit |
|---|---|
| Gives up easily | 1. Set up situations to illustrate to your child that effort produces results.<br>2. Discuss successful people with ADHD and strategies they used to help themselves.<br>3. Develop strategies for motivation when setbacks occur. For example, your child could recall times when "the going was tough" and she did not quit.<br>4. Praise effort more than results.<br>5. Model perseverance in your own daily life.<br>6. Assign and help your child follow through on chores. Some incentives may be necessary initially, but hopefully the big takeaway will be the satisfaction that comes from helping create a functional home environment. |
| Isn't motivated | 1. Make sure your child has an array of tasks within his ability level so he can experience the "taste" of success. For example, if he wants to become better at a sport or at reading, help him realize the benefits of practice.<br>2. Help your child see activities as opportunities for development and not as measures of his worth or capability.<br>3. Have your child think about activities that are motivating for him and how he might use some of that knowledge to motivate himself in other areas. |
| Doesn't appreciate goal-setting—can't set small goals and work toward them | 1. Have your child talk about decisions she has made, strategies or steps used to make the decisions, and the outcomes.<br>2. Give your child practice in breaking large goals down into small manageable steps. For example, making a kite could entail looking up a how-to video, planning the design, purchasing the materials, assembling, and then flying the kite. |
| Doesn't develop or pursue an interest for any period of time | 1. Continue to expose your child to experiences and subject matter that might be an appropriate passion until he latches on to something he enjoys and likes to pursue. Use judgment with computers and especially with video games.<br>2. Encourage reading about people who have pursued interests similar or related to your child's. |

- *Grit for Kids: 16 Top Steps for Developing Grit, Passion, Willpower, and Perseverance in Kids for Self-Confidence and a Successful Life* by Lee David Daniels
- *Raising Children With Grit: Parenting Passionate, Persistent, and Successful Kids* by Laila Y. Sanguras

Useful online resources include Character Lab (available at: https://www.characterlab.org), which provides research-based approaches to developing character strengths, like perseverance.

**Possible careers for adults with strengths or weaknesses in grit.** Adults with strengths in the area of grit have incredible determination and passion for their field of endeavor. Often they are entrepreneurs who start and run successful companies. Many are researchers or doctors who dogmatically pursue cures for diseases, or social workers, teachers, or others in the nonprofit arena who are passionate about improving conditions for people. Many artists and tradespeople are passionate about their craft and pursue it in spite of many obstacles.

Adults with weaknesses in the area of grit would do better in jobs in which production is tightly controlled, like working on an automated factory line, or any job in which the demands are few and expectations are clearly laid out and monitored.

**Example of someone who overcame difficulties with grit.** Jenna Knight is an ADHD coach who works with the Massachusetts Statewide Rehabilitation Council in Boston, MA, and started her own firm, Never Defeated Coaching (Bailey, 2016). She was diagnosed with ADHD as an adult while enrolled in a community college. Figure 14 details how Knight strengthened her grit skills in order to succeed.

## Organization

**Background information.** Organization is related to how children keep up with their belongings, manage a schedule, and get out the door with all of the necessary materials for an activity. We think of it as the ability to impose order on tools, equipment, and possessions

| Who | Jenna Knight, ADHD coach |
|---|---|
| **Natural Talents** | Interpersonal |
| **Factor(s) That Needed Strengthening** | Grit and organization: Knight recalled having a very difficult time with organization in school. Her mother was asked to come to her classroom to look at how disorganized she was and found half-eaten sandwiches in her desk. As a teen, she became involved with drugs and alcohol and was ultimately placed in foster care. She returned home and finished high school but drifted from job to job (Bailey, 2016). |
| **Key(s) to Success** | Through the LD/ADHD Task Force in Massachusetts, Knight "learned more about ADHD and how to manage symptoms" (Bailey, 2016, para. 5). She had been taking medication but knew that wasn't enough. She met an ADHD coach who helped her. She ultimately found her passion in assisting others in managing the disorder. |
| **Advice** | "Never give up. There is help for you out there" (personal communication, January 3, 2019). |

*Figure 14.* Jenna Knight and strengthening grit.

and store them properly. It's important for your child to understand that organizational abilities have very little to do with intelligence—but that *lack* of organizational abilities can make it harder for him to succeed at school and in life. Unfortunately, organization is often a weakness for people with ADHD. To that end, there have even been books written about organizational skills for the "disorganized" adult mind.

It's pretty obvious that a child isn't going to be able to succeed on a higher level if she can never find a pencil and a piece of paper when she has a good idea. If we can determine how to help the child keep her possessions, school supplies, and sports gear organized, she will better be able to succeed in other areas of life. Like other executive functions, organization can be influenced by genetics, environment, and expectations. There is definitely a personality component to organization. Some people thrive on chaos and love to be surrounded by clutter, while others crave order and neatness. A peek into classrooms will show that organizational skills are also impacted by time and place. Some children are organized at school because of the highly structured environment but are totally disheveled at home in spite of organized parents.

Our focus on organization is not intended for you to try to completely change your child's organizational skills but merely make sure that he doesn't miss opportunities and run into academic difficulties because of disorganization. One of the most important things to know is that the system must be one that makes sense to your child and is user friendly to him. Let's say you design an elaborate color-coded folder system for schoolwork or an excellent LEGO storage system. If your child doesn't understand it and feel it works for him, he will likely not make the effort to use it.

Keep in mind that organizational skills are developmental in nature (see Figure 15). Regardless of age, however, as you are helping your child develop his own organizational skills, remember that the more demanding the task, the more help he may need. Don't underestimate the effort it takes for a disorganized, scattered person to be organized. Mary Anne loves information but is very disorganized—always with piles of papers around. For her, filing something away is a torturous task. Much to her family's delight, she continues to work on finding an organization system that will free her workspace of clutter.

Organization skills research posits that it's important to master one skill before moving onto the next. According to Meltzer (2010), "Schema theory suggests that individuals process complex situations by using their previously encoded general knowledge about similar situations" (p. 89). So, before your preteen is able to grasp everything that goes into organizing her backpack for school, she may just need to work on a system for papers that need to be signed and returned. Before your 6-year-old is able to put all of her toys away, she may need to learn how to separate the blocks from the cuddle toys and the art supplies. As much as possible, break down the bigger task into logical steps. Make sure your child is comfortable with each step along the way, and only then have her move on.

| | |
|---|---|
| Ages 4–5 | ▪ Typically enjoy making a game of tidying up, and recognize that most objects have a proper place.<br>▪ Understand that "like" items are stored together. (For example, socks go in pairs in one drawer, shirts in another.) |
| Ages 6–8 | ▪ May have tendency for hoarding. Able to create special settings for their collections.<br>▪ Understand the value of maintaining an organized school backpack or desk, but still need help accomplishing this. |
| Ages 9–12 | ▪ Able to help establish their own practices for organizing their possessions. Should be able to make decisions about what's worth keeping. On the upper end of this age range, can become involved in the care of their own possessions (like maintaining sports equipment or doing their own laundry). |

*Figure 15.* Guidelines for organizational skill development. From *The Impulsive, Disorganized Child: Solutions for Parenting Kids With Executive Functioning Difficulties* (p. 125), by J. W. Forgan and M. A. Richey, 2015, Waco, TX: Prufrock Press. Copyright 2015 by Prufrock Press. Reprinted with permission.

**How weaknesses in organization appear in children.** A child with issues with organization can't keep up with belongings or manage time. His belongings may be scattered all over the house, his backpack may be stuffed with papers, and he may constantly miss deadlines and be late for appointments.

**Strategies for strengthening organization skills.** A big part of helping your child get organized will revolve around establishing routines and good habits at home. Kids need lots of repetition. Repeating behaviors leads to establishing habits, whether they're good or bad. If your kids are anything like our kids, a lot of the time they just want to know "why"—in this case, why they have to take the time to organize themselves and their possessions. There are lots of reasons, from efficiency at homework time, to having a clean and safe living environment, to being able to find their favorite toy when they want it. At home, organizational challenges affect two major areas—homework and a child's living space.

Let's talk about homework first. Krishnan and Meltzer (2014) described that "a common complaint of many children is that they don't have time to do the things they want to do" because their homework is so time-consuming (para. 13). As the parent, you can encourage and motivate your child when you emphasize that the *reason* you want to help him become an organized person is that having a system will make his life easier. Remember, your child thinks that organization is hard. You must show that there's a payoff, including:

- homework going more smoothly,
- feeling less stress and pressure, and
- being able to spend more time doing what she wants to do.

*A big part of helping your child get organized will revolve around establishing routines and good habits at home.*

You probably already know the value of designating a quiet, clutter-free, distraction-free area for your child to do schoolwork. For younger children, it's especially helpful to have a "homework box" that contains pencils, pens, erasers, lined paper—whatever supplies your child regularly needs at homework time. Help her understand that it's a personal responsibility to get the box out, lay out the items needed that day, replace them when homework is done, and return the box to its proper place. Not only does this help reduce the amount of time your child spends looking for the tools needed to complete homework, but also it provides practice in organization every time she uses the box. Older children can successfully use this system as well. Many preteens have their own desks in their bedrooms, but we all know how hard it is to keep a desk organized. It's much easier to organize one box or drawer. The desk can come later, and for some of us, it never really comes at all.

When it comes to helping your child with his room, don't assume for a minute that he has any idea of how to organize the space. Start small. Take your child on a tour of your own bedroom and show how you've decided to arrange it, and why. Explain everything, from why you put your wallet in your sock drawer ("I always know how to find it, and it's out of sight") to why the bathroom towels go in the bathroom linen closet ("You put towels close to where you need them"). Take a tour through other areas of the house and talk about other organizational systems. Your keys and sunglasses always go in the same spot. Why? You never have to hunt for them. The location doesn't necessarily matter, as long as it's meaningful to *you*. Ask your child for any suggestions for how your home may be better organized, and consider implementing some of his ideas. It's a powerful thing when a kid gets the chance to instruct an adult. Be willing to be taught by your child if organization is also a challenge for you.

Now, tour your child's bedroom and/or bathroom. Talk about making the space functional—after all, that's the point of organization. Go through each drawer, being willing to rearrange them if your child feels better able to manage a different setup. There is no point insisting the socks go in the upper left-hand drawer if he wants them in a lower drawer because they're closer to his feet.

Remind your child that a neat room and an organized room are not necessarily the same thing. If your child's space appears to be tidy but he still can't find anything because everything is shoved into drawers and under the bed, it's not organized. By the same token, if his room looks messy to you but makes sense to him and allows him to find what he needs, he's found a functional system. Take things slowly. Here are a couple of suggestions:

- Many children enjoy collections. Managing their collections gives them great practice in thinking through how it will be organized, displayed, and stored. It doesn't seem like work because the things they collect are interesting to them.
- Assign your children household chores that remind them everything has its place. Young children may help you put away laundry or help you sort the mail. Older children could empty the dishwasher, which will help them see how your kitchen is organized and get them in the habit of putting things back in the same place every time.

Table 19 is a list of further strategies for strengthening your child's organization skills.

**Resources for strengthening organization skills.** Books for children include:

- *Wyatt the Wonder Dog Learns About Being Organized* by Lynne Watts (ages 5 and older)
- *Annie's Plan: Taking Charge of Schoolwork and Homework* by Jeanne R. Kraus (ages 7 and older)
- *Learning to Plan and Be Organized: Executive Function Skills for Kids With ADHD* by Kathleen Nadeau (ages 8–12)
- *Get Organized Without Losing It* by Janet S. Fox (ages 8–13)

Books for adults include:

- *The Crumpled Paper Was Due Last Week: Helping Disorganized and Distracted Boys Succeed in Life* by Ana Homayoun
- *The Impulsive, Disorganized Child: Solutions for Parenting Kids With Executive Functioning Difficulties* by James W. Forgan and Mary Anne Richey

Useful devices and apps include:

- Amazon Echo Dot Kid Edition ($80): Allows children to set alarms for waking up, brushing teeth, getting dressed and more.
- Cozi Family Organizer (free)
- The Homework App
- myHomework Student Planner
- OurHome: Chores and Rewards
- Power Planner (free): A Windows app available from the Microsoft Store that syncs with iOS and Android

**Possible careers for adults with strengths or weaknesses in organization.** Adults who possess good organizational skills are often detail-oriented and good at planning, and like order. Many of the trades, such as plumbing, construction, and appliance repair, require people who can meet schedules and keep required materials on hand.

*Table 19*
Strategies for Strengthening Your Child's Organization

| Characteristics | Activities to Strengthen Organization |
|---|---|
| Doesn't gather proper materials for the task | 1. Help your child create a homework box with pencils, pencil sharpener, pens, erasers, markers, lined paper, sticky notes, calculator, ruler, or any supplies needed for homework.<br>2. When leaving for an activity, help your child learn to visualize everything he will need and pack it all in a bag.<br>3. Try to have a specific place for every item. For example, school backpacks should be placed by the door. |
| Doesn't make or follow a schedule | 1. For younger children, make a picture schedule of morning or evening routines. Some children enjoy photographs of themselves doing the activity, like brushing teeth.<br>2. For older children, make a written schedule and have them check off the task when completed. |
| Doesn't meet deadlines | 1. Teach time management and the ability to estimate how long various activities will take. (See Figure 7, p. 85.)<br>2. When given a large project, help your child develop a process that involves entering the due date on a calendar and then working backward, allotting time each day for a small portion of the project.<br>3. For older children, use a digital calendar, such as Google Calendar or Cozi Family Organizer, to keep track of family activities and commitments.<br>4. For older children, work with them to come up with consequences for missing deadlines.<br>5. For older children, help them develop a habit of checking their school's daily grade reporting system. |
| Has a disorderly room | 1. Help your child break down the task into manageable pieces. Children younger than 5 or 6 will need even more support.<br>2. Make sure there is adequate storage.<br>3. Have natural consequences, such as if dirty clothes aren't in the laundry hamper, then the child must launder them. |

Anyone in management usually has good organizational skills or the ability to delegate to someone who does. Engineers, architects, and accountants are usually well-organized.

People who are weak in organizational skills would do better in an environment in which organization is imposed on them, such as being on a factory assembly line, working in a restaurant, or working in an office where they have specified tasks.

**Example of someone who managed difficulties with organization.** Selim Bassoul is CEO of Middleby Corporation, a kitchen supply manufacturer, and head of the Bassoul Dignity Foundation, which helps refugees with vocational training programs. He was diagnosed with ADHD and dyslexia as a graduate student (Silverman, 2017). Figure 16 details how Bassoul strengthened his organizational skills in order to succeed.

## Resilience

Resilience involves the ability to bounce back after a disappointment or tragedy. It is "a varied and dynamic mix of many traits like determination, toughness, optimism, faith, positivity and hope" (Jamieson, 2018). On a daily basis, resilience involves the ability to be flexible and adjust to change. As with organization, there is definitely a personality component involved. We know children who are very rigid and freak out when the day does not unfold as they expected and those who "go with the flow." Seeing the world in black and white with little room for ambiguity feeds into a child having a lack of resilience.

Although we are not suggesting you can change your child's temperament, remember that your child is also influenced by experiences in the environment. Resilience has been likened to a muscle—the more you use it, the stronger it grows. Resiliency "is something you can foster in your children by exposing them to change and giving them tools to cope with it" (Forgan & Richey, 2015, p. 81). Other factors that promote resilience include:

- close, supportive relationships, which could come from parents, grandparents, other relatives, teachers, or community members;
- positive parenting skills;
- development of a sense of purpose, which could come from identity, culture, community, or faith;
- social connectedness; and

| Who | Selim Bassoul, CEO |
|---|---|
| **Natural Talents** | Logical and Interpersonal |
| **Factor(s) That Needed Strengthening** | Organization: Bassoul was diagnosed with ADHD and dyslexia while in graduate school. He realized his brain wasn't at its best when bogged down with administrative tasks and keeping details organized, so he minimized those and spends time in the factory or with his sales force. He noted that his impatience with time wasted in meetings led him to cut back on meetings in his company. |
| **Key(s) to Success** | Bassoul is a big picture thinker who doesn't allow himself to get mired in details. He noted that he has become a good judge of character because he has had to rely on the help of others. He is very goal-oriented and focused on the bottom line of his company. His flexibility has enabled him to implement a leadership style that fits with his strengths and weaknesses. |
| **Advice** | "I want to give people hope that there is an alternative way of managing. That someone like me can be successful and accepted." |

*Figure 16.* Selim Bassoul and strengthening organization skills (Silverman, 2017).

- personal characteristics, such as emotional regulation, optimism, hope, and having a growth mindset, which is built on seeing a situation as an opportunity to practice and improve, not as a measure of one's worth.

Ginsburg and Jablow (2011) studied resilience in children extensively and identified the Seven Crucial C's of Resilience as:
1. competence,
2. confidence,
3. connection,
4. character,
5. contribution,
6. coping, and
7. control (p. 24).

**How weaknesses in resilience appear in children.** A child with deficits in this area is inflexible and melts down when faced with a challenge. She may become very upset when schedules change or when things don't unfold as planned. She may be easily derailed by failure, find it hard to maintain an even disposition, and have difficulty regaining momentum.

**Strategies for strengthening resilience.** Resilience has to do with shifting and being flexible by changing how you think about things. A child who displays "all or nothing" thinking has much more trouble moving past a problem than a child who can look for any positive in the situation and move on from there to make a better plan. Obsessing over things that didn't work out is wasted energy that could be better used toward working for a better outcome in the future. Of course, your child may feel frustration and disappointment, but these can be expressed in an appropriate manner and can even be useful in motivation to seek a better outcome next time. As a parent, you don't want to jump in and save your child from disappointment because that will ultimately lead her to believe she is not capable or cannot solve problems on her own. You want to be supportive as she works through a problem to a solution. Lack of resilience is a hallmark of conditions like autism spectrum disorders and obsessive-compulsive disorder. If your child suffers from one of these conditions, encouraging resilience will likely require professional support.

Table 20 is a list of strategies for strengthening resilience in your child.

**Resources for strengthening resilience.** Books for children include:

- *The Name Jar* by Yangsook Choi (ages 3–7)
- *The Hugging Tree: A Story About Resilience* by Jill Neimark (ages 4–8)
- *A Happy Hat* by Cecil Kim (ages 4–8)
- *Stickley Makes a Mistake!: A Frog's Guide to Trying Again* by Brenda S. Miles (ages 4–8)
- *The Short Tree and the Bird That Could Not Sing* by Dennis Foon (ages 6–10)

# Keys to Success

*Table 20*

Strategies for Strengthening Your Child's Resilience

| Characteristics | Activities to Strengthen Resilience |
|---|---|
| Doesn't bounce back from failure | 1. Help your child learn to accurately identify feelings and then verbalize them appropriately.<br>2. Reinforce the concept that failure is a very important part of learning.<br>3. Help your child identify activities or thoughts that help her return to equilibrium, like yoga, breathing, visualizing, looking at books, etc.<br>4. Reinforce the concept of gratitude and being grateful for what has gone right during the day or week. |
| Doesn't seem to learn from mistakes | 1. Some children are so anxious and fearful of mistakes that they aren't free to learn from them; they try to forget about them. When they are calm, help them see mistakes can be corrected. Encourage them to express what they might do differently next time.<br>2. Don't criticize mistakes made by your child.<br>3. Help your child engage in positive self-talk and plan for a next time. For example, if they bring the wrong things to sports practice, they could say, "I'll do better next time by putting everything I need in my gym bag and putting it by the door."<br>4. Model making mistakes in your life and verbalize what you learned from them to help you do better next time. |
| Doesn't seem to have a sense of belonging to any group (e.g., team, friends or classroom) | 1. In the classroom, talk with the teacher to ask for help in assisting your child to make connections.<br>2. For younger children, if possible, volunteer in the classroom or with school activities to try to identify children who might have things in common with your child.<br>3. Continually try to help your child identify a group to join, whether it is a club at school or in the community.<br>4. Make sure your child is not spending so much time on video games or online that it begins to interfere with socializing with others. |
| Isn't resilient | 1. Try not to let your child develop habits that are too rigid, such as having to have a certain breakfast food every day.<br>2. Provide advance warning for changes, such as a 5-minute warning before putting away an activity.<br>3. Point out and praise your child's resiliency when you observe it.<br>4. Let your child help you reschedule an activity when it has to be postponed.<br>5. Implement changes that could be fun, like changing the rules of a game. |

- *Bounce Back: How to Be a Resilient Kid* by Wendy L. Moss (ages 8–12)
- *Nothing You Can't Do!: The Secret Power of Growth Mindsets* by Mary Cay Ricci (ages 9–12)

Games for children include:
- Solution City (ages 8–15): Provides practice in problem solving: https://www.playtherapysupply.com/games/solution-city-board-game

Books for adults include:
- *Never Give Up (Building Resilience and Persistence in Kids)* by Cally and Timothy Finsbury
- *Building Resilience in Children and Teens: Giving Kids Roots and Wings* (3rd ed.) by Kenneth R. Ginsburg with Martha Jablow
- *The Yes Brain: How to Cultivate Courage, Curiosity, and Resilience in Your Child* by Daniel Siegel and Tina Bryson
- *Mindset: The New Psychology of Success* by Carol S. Dweck
- *Mindsets for Parents: Strategies to Encourage Growth Mindsets in Kids* by Mary Cay Ricci and Margaret Lee

Some online resources and apps include:
- Reaching In . . . Reaching Out (available at http://reaching inreachingout.com): Provides evidence-based resources for teaching resiliency to children under 8 years.
- Tiny Rabbit: Chasing Auroa (free game for iOS): Features a rabbit who learns by trial and error.
- "Tipping the Scales: The Resilience Game" (available at https://developingchild.harvard.edu/resources/resilience-game) is an interactive, browser-based game.
- "4 Resilience Building Games for Kids in Primary School" (available at https://positivepsychologyprogram.com/resilience-activities-worksheets/#kids-resilience): Features games that teach kids resilience, kindness, and how to deal with conflict.

**Possible careers for adults with strengths or weaknesses in resilience.** Adults who are strong in resilience would be assets in fields in which the outcome is often out of their control, like being a realtor, or areas like construction, interior design, advertising, or business contracting, in which projects are bid on and the customer decides which bid to accept.

Adults who continue to be weak in resilience might be more successful in careers that offer predictability and routine. For example, careers like stocking shelves, filling orders at warehouses, or landscaping, or health care jobs that are routine, like being a phlebotomist.

**Example of someone who overcame difficulties with resilience.** Toya Haynes is a freelance writer, concert producer, and events coordinator, who was diagnosed with ADHD at age 41 (Kaleidoscope Society, 2016). Figure 17 details how Haynes strengthened her resilience.

## *Resourcefulness*

**Background information.** Resourcefulness is based in problem solving and involves being able to pull together things needed to accomplish a task or reach a goal. Resourcefulness is especially useful when things don't go as planned. It often involves acting imaginatively to develop unique solutions to a problem. In today's complex world, resourcefulness can't be ignored. It will certainly be a valuable tool for your child as he navigates some of the difficulties related to ADHD.

Children with ADHD are notorious for forgetting things or losing belongings. If your child forgets a book needed for a class test, he must problem solve how to get a book to use. Your child could ask the teacher early in the day if she has an extra one, borrow one from another student, ask to take the test as a make-up, or, as a last resort, ask a parent to bring the book. If you remember the TV character Angus MacGyver, you will recall he was masterful at being resourceful. He used unconventional problem-solving skills to save lives. We want our children to learn to use all of the tools at their disposal to face problems in a creative and adaptive way. When confronted by a wall,

| Who | Toya Haynes, Freelance writer |
|---|---|
| **Natural Talents** | Interpersonal |
| **Factor(s) That Needed Strengthening** | Resilience: For years, Haynes felt like an "invisible wall" was keeping her from being successful. She continually felt that she was letting other people down. After suffering depression as she neared middle age, she moved back to live with her parents to try to make sense of her difficulties. She began to research ADHD after hearing about it from a friend and ultimately was diagnosed by a psychiatrist: "My self-esteem took such a terrible beating for so many years because I didn't understand why I was having the challenges that come with having ADHD" (para. 7). |
| **Key(s) to Success** | Haynes said her life completely changed when she was diagnosed with ADHD, understood how the frustrations in her life were related to the disorder, received treatment, and became aware of how successful people coped with ADHD: "I'm currently healing from that, thank God. I've decided to love myself extra hard now to make up for all those years" (para. 7). |
| **Advice** | "There's no need to be in denial about your challenges. Do what you have to do for YOU and make it fun! Yes, ADHD is exhausting at times but it can also be a big colorful life that never has a dull moment" (para. 5). |

*Figure 17.* Toya Haynes and strengthening resiliency (Kaleidoscope Society, 2016).

we want our children to be able to figure a way around it, under it, or over it, but not give up and walk away.

The old saying "Necessity is the mother of invention" comes to mind. To put it in simple terms, "Resourcefulness = Necessity + Creativity + Persistence" (Marrero, 2018). If you have ever been stuck in an airport during inclement weather with all flights cancelled for the rest of the day, you fared much better if you were resourceful. You might have booked a nearby hotel, made a comfortable place to sleep in a corner of the terminal, or arranged alternate transportation, such as a train or rental car. In order to do that, you had to access information and probably relied on help from others.

**How weaknesses in resourcefulness appear in children.** A child who has deficits in this area is not a problem solver and doesn't think of ways to resolve situations that arise. A child who lacks resourcefulness will often be stonewalled when things don't go as planned and will have difficulty thinking of alternative solutions to problems.

**Strategies for strengthening resourcefulness.** Children who are resourceful are good problem solvers. When one thing doesn't work out, they can substitute another idea. They generally are easily able to draw on working memory to think of previous experiences and knowledge to help in coming up with new ideas. People often call them outside-of-the-box thinkers. They are usually able to stay calm under pressure to enable their prefrontal cortex to call on multiple areas of the brain to figure out solutions and new directions.

Involve your child in generating solutions to complex problems, helping her think through the pros and cons of various solutions in a nonjudgmental, supportive way. Teach your child to ask herself questions, such as "Who else might have information I can use?" or "What is one more thing I can try?" Table 21 is a list of further strategies for strengthening resourcefulness in your child.

**Possible careers for adults with strengths or weaknesses in resourcefulness.** Adults who are strong in resourcefulness would be assets in fields requiring problem solving, such as engineering, architecture, plant management, teaching, construction trades, psychology, or medicine. News reporters are resourceful in pursuing leads for stories.

Adults who continue to be weak in resourcefulness might be more successful in careers that offer routine and consistency and someone above them to solve problems and make adjustments. For example, careers involving stocking shelves, routine maintenance, and standardized appliance or device repair might be appropriate.

**Resources for strengthening resourcefulness.** Books for children include:

- *Little Blue Truck* by Alice Schertle (ages 2–4)
- *The Monster Returns* by Peter McCarty (ages 3–6)

*Table 21*
Strategies for Strengthening Your Child's Resourcefulness

| Characteristics | Activities to Strengthen Resourcefulness |
|---|---|
| Is inflexible in thinking | 1. For younger children, provide opportunities for open-ended play.<br>2. Create opportunities for children to solve their own problems and have plenty of time to test out possible solutions and ideas.<br>3. Practice trial-and-error learning, like Sudoku, or games where you have to take chances, like chess. |
| Doesn't seem to see the "big picture" in a situation and is unable to take on different roles | 1. Talk through planning, such as packing for a trip and point out the "big picture" so the family will have what they need.<br>2. Relate chores to the "big picture"—dividing the trash into recyclables leads to less trash in the landfills.<br>3. Talk through situations; explain what is expected and why it is important. |
| Doesn't think of alternative solutions | 1. Engage your child in generating solutions to everyday problems.<br>2. Use everyday household items in different ways. For example, build a fort from couch cushions, use a large book as a booster seat, or play drums on pots and pans.<br>3. When watching a movie or reading a story, point out and discuss situations in which characters had to come up with new solutions to problems faced. |
| Has difficulty adjusting to new or difficult situations | 1. Prepare your child ahead of time for what to expect. Brainstorm with her what might help her feel more comfortable.<br>2. When a situation doesn't work out as expected, help your child plan a replacement activity. For example, if it rains and he can't go swimming, set a new time to go and try to come up with a fun, alternative activity for the rainy day.<br>3. Remind your child of new situations in which everything worked out fine. |

- *Extra Yarn* by Mac Barnett (ages 4–8)
- *One Cool Friend* by Toni Buzzeo (ages 5–8)
- *A Chair for My Mother* by Vera B. Williams (ages 5–10)

Books for adults include *365 Ways to Help Your Children Grow* by Sheila Ellison.

Some online resources include:

- "Resourcefulness: How Parents Help Children Achieve Goals" by Marilyn Price-Mitchell (available at https://www.rootsof action.com/resourcefulness-children): Provides 11 ways to foster resourcefulness in children.
- "3 Skills That Teach Resourcefulness" by Michele Borba (available at https://www.micheleborba.com/how-to-raise-a-self-reliant-kid-part-i): Describes three essential skills to instill in children in order to build resourcefulness.
- "Resourcefulness Activities for Kids" by Rosenya Faith (available at https://howtoadult.com/560600-resourcefulness-activities-for-kids.html): Includes five activities to cultivating resourcefulness in children.
- "20 Ways to Encourage Children's Resourcefulness and Creativity" by Karen Stephens (available at https://dcf.wisconsin.gov/files/ccic/pdf/articles/twenty-ways-to-encourage-childrens-resourcefulness.pdf): Features a comprehensive list of ways to encourage creativity and resourcefulness in kids.

**Example of someone who overcame difficulties with resourcefulness.** Even Polk Green is a project director at Illinois STAR Net (a group providing training to parents and educators) and former president of the Attention Deficit Disorder Association. She was diagnosed as an adult when one of her sons was being diagnosed (personal communication, 2014). Figure 18 details how Green strengthened her resourcefulness skills.

# External Keys to Success

## Appropriate School Setting

**Background information.** The average American school student has 900–1,000 hours of instructional time per year spread over 180 days (Center for Public Education, 2011). As difficult as assessing

| Who | Even Polk Green, Project Director |
|---|---|
| **Natural Talents** | Interpersonal |
| **Factor(s) That Needed Strengthening** | Resourcefulness, organization, and support systems: Green was very successful in high school when she also worked part-time. She flourished in a structured environment with support and earned a scholarship to Duke University. At that time, there were only 100 African American students on campus, so she was often the only person of color in her classes. She struggled with the shift in culture and socioeconomic status of those around her and couldn't figure out how to be successful in her new environment. She had to leave Duke without graduating, had a child, and then went back to school while holding down a full-time job. She realized she was able to hyperfocus to meet deadlines but had trouble managing the day-to-day responsibilities of running her household. When her son was being diagnosed with ADHD, she realized her difficulties matched the disorder, was diagnosed, and started medication to improve her focus. |
| **Key(s) to Success** | "I'm not really sure how I found my passion, but I think that a large part of it had to do with wanting to make life better for others. In my work life, that means helping families of young children learn and know all of the skills they need to be successful (especially young kids with special needs). With the ADHD and mental health advocacy work, I think it's all about giving back—so many people helped me on my journey, I feel it is my responsibility to do the same for others." |
| **Advice** | "I think if I'd just known I had the disorder, it could have made a huge difference for me. I went the first 30 odd years of my life feeling out of step with the rest of the world and usually angry with myself for not 'living up to my potential.' Realizing there was a reason for all of the things that were 'wrong' with me, was an incredibly liberating experience." |

*Figure 18.* Even Polk Green and strengthening resourcefulness (personal communication, 2014).

school fit might be, it is important to spend the time to ensure that your child is in a setting that recognizes her worth as an individual and provides an appropriate educational program. In our practice, we have seen both sides—how devastating a negative school experience can be and how an appropriate, positive one can turn a child's attitude toward learning completely around.

There are several components to a good fit. First of all, a school needs to be a place where your child feels safe and valued. Most of us have concerns these days about school safety. It breaks our hearts that students need to practice active shooter drills, but that is our reality. You need to feel that the school is taking reasonable safety precautions and has emergency plans, but also tries to make your child feel secure.

> *A school needs to be a place where your child feels safe and valued.*

We have found that the principal sets the tone of the school as the instructional leader. It is important for you to feel that the school is well-run, focuses on what is important, and has the students' best interest at heart. Some principals have an open-door policy, whereas others have other administrative staff handle parent concerns. It is important that you have a responsive communication link with the school.

In terms of instruction, a program that differentiates instruction enough to keep your child challenged, but not overwhelmed, is ideal. By differentiation of instruction we mean that the school can tailor the curriculum to meet your child's needs. If your child is reading below grade level, today's reading curricula provide a variety of materials so that it is easier for teachers to have children reading at their level so that their skills can grow. We have seen many children shut down because the material they were given was too difficult or easy for them.

Many of our students with ADHD have needs that transcend academics. It is helpful if they can connect with the teacher on a human level. We all know that some teachers are much more knowledgeable about ADHD than others and more able to handle the problems that ADHD may bring to the classroom. The relationship children have with their teacher can be crucial. It is important for children to learn to deal with all different types of personalities, but some of our students with ADHD aren't ready for that challenge and need more support than a stern, rigid teacher may be willing to provide. If your child doesn't connect with her teacher, try to find someone else in the school who believes in your child and provides encouragement. Every child needs someone who values and believes in her.

Peer interactions are also important. If your child has no friends, is alone at lunch or recess, or even worse, is bullied, school can be a miserable experience. These kinds of social issues can lead to depression and a host of other school-related problems. Try to figure out why your child doesn't have friends. Some children lack social skills, others are shy, and some prefer to be alone. Consult with the school's guidance counselor or your child's teacher to try to help your child establish some social contacts. If there are any incidents of bullying, make sure to alert school staff. Most schools take bullying very seriously. Communicate openly with your child about bullying because you want him to be comfortable confiding in you if it is happening. The following website has information for parents: https://www.stop bullying.gov.

**How difficulty with school fit may appear.** Your child may be having difficulties with school fit if he is in a school setting where expectations are unrealistic given his skills and he is not a valued member of the school community. A child who is not receiving appropriate instruction to advance his skills can easily become demoralized and give up.

**Strategies for strengthening school fit.** Table 22 is a list of strategies for improving your child's school fit. However, if you feel your child's current school is just not the right fit and no adjustments will make a difference, note that alternative school options are discussed in Chapter 7.

# Keys to Success

*Table 22*
Strategies for Improving Your Child's School Fit

| Characteristics | Activities to Strengthen School Fit |
|---|---|
| The school doesn't seem to recognize your child's academic needs and/or doesn't follow the 504 plan/IEP | 1. Make a brief list of your child's strengths and weaknesses to share with the teachers.<br>2. If your child has an IEP or 504 plan, set up a meeting with the school staff to review it. Remind the school that it is a legal document and must be followed.<br>3. If the school still doesn't follow it, seek the services of a parent advocate, a school district employee in an advisory capacity, or an attorney specializing in special education law.<br>4. If all efforts fail, it may be time to consider another school. |
| Academic work far exceeds your child's skill level | 1. Ask for a meeting with the teacher to find out how the instruction can be differentiated to provide work on your child's level.<br>2. Find out how you can support your child at home by working with your child or providing private tutoring.<br>3. If your child has an IEP, make sure goals are specific about skill level and criteria about how improvement will be monitored. Sometimes careful monitoring of progress can encourage teachers to be more diligent. |
| Your child doesn't have friends and/or is socially ostracized | 1. Communicate with the teacher(s) to find out their assessment of the situation.<br>2. If your child lacks social skills or is engaging in some behaviors that annoy others, working with the school guidance counselor or a private therapist outside of school might be helpful.<br>3. For younger children, try to arrange playdates with classmates. If your child is shy, have structured activities like bowling, going to a movie, or a bounce activity center.<br>4. For older children, try involving them in an extracurricular activity where they can meet people who may have similar interests.<br>5. If an IEP is in place, add a social goal to address a deficit, like making eye contact or initiating conversations with other students. |
| School environment is negative and punitive | 1. Have a conference with the teacher to try to determine the source of the negativity.<br>2. If it appears to be schoolwide, set up a conference with the principal.<br>3. Try involving the PTA if one is active. Some possibilities could be sponsoring a speaker to talk to the faculty about the benefits of a positive learning environment for teachers and students. Many local psychologists will speak to school groups for free. |

**Resources for strengthening school fit.** Books for children include:

- *Oh No, School!* by Hae-Kyung Chang (ages 3–6)
- *Some Days Are Lonely* by Young-Ah Kim (ages 4–8)
- *School Made Easier: A Kid's Guide to Study Strategies and Anxiety-Busting Tools* by Wendy L. Moss and Robin DeLuca-Acconi (ages 9–13)

Books for adults include:

- *The Power of Parents: A Critical Perspective of Bicultural Parent Involvement in Public Schools* by Edward M. Olivos
- *Parents as Partners in Education: Families and Schools Working Together* (9th ed.) by Eugenia Hepworth Berger and Mari Riojas-Cortez
- *Schools: How Parents Can Make a Difference* by Ethel Herr
- *Making the Most of Middle School: A Field Guide for Parents and Others* by Anthony Jackson, P. Gayle Andrews, Holly Holland, and Priscilla Pardini
- *The Genius in Every Child: Encouraging Character, Curiosity, and Creativity in Children* by Rick Ackerly
- *Raising Boys With ADHD: Secrets for Parenting Healthy, Happy Sons* by James W. Forgan and Mary Anne Richey
- *Raising Girls With ADHD: Secrets for Parenting Healthy, Happy Daughters* by James W. Forgan and Mary Anne Richey

Some useful online resources include:

- "How to Choose a School" by PBS Parents (available at http://www.pbs.org/parents/education/going-to-school/choosing): Provides tips for selecting play-based versus academic preschools, choosing elementary or middle schools, and more.
- "Free Parent Resources" by Discovery Education (available at http://www.discoveryeducation.com/parents/?campaign=-flyout_parents): Offers homework help, video tutorials on a variety of subjects, and other free resources.

- "Homework Center" by Infoplease (available at https://www.infoplease.com/homework): Provides facts and other information separated by subject.
- "Websites That Help Kids Succeed in School" by Ellen Ullman (available at https://www.techlicious.com/website/websites-that-help-kids-succeed-in-school): Provides a list of tips for determining if a website is a good source as well as a list of resources broken down by subject area.

**How school setting impacts adult careers.** Adults who had appropriate school settings probably developed many skills to help them make the most of their abilities, especially knowledge of their own strengths and weaknesses and how to accommodate them. Careers would be based on their capabilities.

Adults who had academic settings that didn't match their abilities probably have much weaker skills development than they would have otherwise. They may end up being underemployed and have difficulty developing their strengths to the fullest. However, sometimes people develop their talents in spite of having a poor fit in their educational life.

**Example of someone who felt his academic setting was not appropriate.** Channing Tatum is an actor who has been in hit films, including *21 Jump Street*, *Step Up*, *The LEGO Movie*, *Magic Mike*, and *White House Down*. He was diagnosed with ADHD as a child (Haskell, 2014). Figure 19 details how Tatum found a way to learn.

## Support Systems

**Background information.** Support systems can be invaluable to you and your child with ADHD. They can come in a variety of forms—from teachers, to tutors, to behavior therapists, and more. Don't try to go alone on your journey of bringing up a successful child with ADHD. Help along the way could make things so much easier for you and your child and result in better outcomes.

| Who | Channing Tatum, Actor |
|---|---|
| **Natural Talents** | Interpersonal and Bodily-Kinesthetic |
| **Factor(s) That Needed Strengthening** | Appropriate school setting: Tatum's school experience in a small Southern town was not positive. He was diagnosed with ADHD and dyslexia. He took stimulants and was placed in special education classes. He felt like a misfit in both special education and regular classes: "You're kind of nowhere. You're just different. The system is broken. If we can streamline a multibillion-dollar company, we should be able to help kids who struggle the way I did" (para. 3). |
| **Key(s) to Success** | Tatum was voted most athletic in high school, so his involvement in sports was likely a positive for him. He received a football scholarship to college but was not successful there. Later, he discovered an interest in the arts, especially acting. He marveled that given his struggles in school, no one pushed him toward the arts; "So when I started going out in the world, I was drawn to people who knew about movies, art, even fashion. . . . I just learned everything I could from anybody who knew something I didn't. . . I can look at a person and say, they've got something that I want up there in their head. I'm going to do my best to get in there and absorb it" (para. 8). In addition to acting and modeling, he now enjoys sculpting. |
| **Advice** | Schools need to be pushed to do a better job in meeting the needs of those who learn differently. |

*Figure 19.* Channing Tatum and school setting (Haskell, 2014).

In biographies of successful people from many different walks of life who have overcome some type of difficulty, the single factor that stands out is that they had someone who believed in them and encouraged them to be the best they could be. We know when you are in the trenches, it feels like it would be easier to give up and just let history take its course, but we are here to tell you that your efforts are invaluable. Think about the negative comments directed to your child with ADHD, like "You're just not trying to remember," or "You're just lazy."

If your child receives messages like these, he or she can easily start believing those messages and just give up.

David Neeleman, founder of JetBlue, suggested that his creativity and the ability to take risks are related to his ADHD. In an interview with *ADDitude* magazine (Gilman 2004/2005), Neeleman said:

> I knew I had strengths that other people didn't have, and my parents reminded me of them when my teachers didn't see them. I can distill complicated facts and come up with simple solutions. I can look out on an industry with all kinds of problems and say, "How can I do this better?" My ADHD brain naturally searches for better ways of doing things. (para. 8)

One tricky aspect of providing support is that it is critical to determine when a situation is a "can't" or "won't" issue. You don't want your child to become too dependent on you as a support person and develop learned helplessness in which the motivation to do things is lost. It is very important to evaluate your child's skills and determine when she has the skills to do things on her own and when she needs support. We call this *scaffolding*, providing just enough help to accomplish the task and gradually withdrawing the support as skills improve. For example, if your child has a big project to do for school, he may be overwhelmed and not have the executive functioning skills necessary to break the job down into manageable parts. Scaffolding in this example might involve helping your child record the due date on a calendar and then planning backward, deciding what part of the job would be done each day.

When you feel the help your child needs exceeds your own skills, it is time to consider outside support. Many children with ADHD benefit from coaching, especially to address their executive functioning skills. If there are no ADHD coaches in your area, many coaches work remotely via Skype or other remote video technology. If the problems are mostly academic, private tutors can be very effective in helping your child catch up on missing skills. If behavior is the main problem, behavior therapists, mental health therapists, or psychologists could be good resources.

**How weaknesses in support systems appear in children.** A child without a support system does not have a "cheerleader" who values and notices his efforts and, in general, "has his back." A child who doesn't have a support system can become discouraged and won't have a relationship with an adult with whom he can confide and ask for support in dealing with problems. An adult supporter who affirms a child's worth can do a lot to counteract the negative messages encountered at school or in other environments in the child's life.

**Strategies for strengthening support systems.** Table 23 is a list of strategies for improving your child's support systems. Note that when your child is mature enough to understand and handle it, helping your child have a clear idea of strengths and areas where help is needed will be important. When it is all said and done, your child will be her best advocate in seeking out necessary supports.

**Resources for strengthening support systems.** Books for children include:

- *How I Learn: A Kid's Guide to Learning Disability* by Brenda Miles and Colleen Patterson (ages 4–8)
- *I Just Want to Do It My Way: My Story About Staying on Task and Asking for Help (Best Me I Can Be! Book 5)* by Julia Cook (ages 5–12)
- *Get Ready for Jetty!: My Journal About ADHD and Me* by Jeanne Kraus (ages 9–12)
- *Putting on the Brakes: Understanding and Taking Control of Your ADD or ADHD* (3rd ed.) by Patricia O. Quinn and Judith M. Stern (ages 8–13)
- *Putting on the Brakes Activity Book for Kids With ADD or ADHD* (2nd ed.) by Patricia O. Quinn and Judith M. Stern (ages 8–13)

Books for adults include:

- *No Regrets Parenting: Turning Long Days and Short Years Into Cherished Moments With Your Kids* by Harley Rotbart

*Table 23*
Strategies for Strengthening Your Child's Support Systems

| Characteristics | Activities to Strengthen Support Systems |
|---|---|
| Does not have anyone who helps bring out the best in him and who believes he can be successful | 1. Keep searching for those positive people who understand ADHD and are able to appreciate strengths in individual areas.<br>2. Educate your family and friends about ADHD. Helping people understand that ADHD is a neurobiological disorder and not a failure of willpower or desire can go a long way.<br>3. Be your child's best cheerleader—perhaps it will be contagious! |
| Does not have any adult who spends quality time with him | 1. If your schedule does not permit quality time daily, even 15 minutes when your child is the focus, try to enlist the support of others—spouses, grandparents, or relatives.<br>2. Consider enrolling your child in a sport or community activity, like Scouts or a church group, where he might find an adult mentor. |
| Does not ask for support when needed | 1. Make sure your child is aware of strengths and areas where support is needed.<br>2. Reinforce the idea that asking for help is not a sign of weakness but a way to gain the ability to be independent and no longer need help.<br>3. Help your child choose the format most comfortable for her to use when asking for help, whether it is a note to the teacher, a private conversation, or an e-mail.<br>4. Role-play with your child situations in which help might be needed and how to approach it. |
| Has teachers who have low expectations and appear to have given up on him | 1. Prepare a brief list of your child's strengths and weaknesses and what helps him to be successful in the classroom. Include any additional things you are willing to do to support him.<br>2. Ask for a conference with the teacher and express your concern in a respectful manner, focusing on how the situation can be improved.<br>3. If no progress is made, ask for a second conference with an administrator present. If it appears the classroom will continue to be demoralizing for your child, request and insist on a teacher change. Schools are sometimes resistive to changing a classroom, but if you don't advocate for your child, who will? As we have noted previously, sometimes an advocate or an attorney will be needed. |

- *Smart Parenting for Smart Kids: Nurturing Your Child's True Potential* by Eileen Kennedy-Moore and Mark S. Lowenthal

Some useful online resources include:
- "4 Ways to Help Your Child Build a Support Network" by Erica Patino (available at https://www.understood.org/en/friends-feelings/empowering-your-child/self-advocacy/4-ways-to-help-your-child-build-a-support-network): Provides four ways for parents to help their children build their own support networks.
- "The Role of Parents" by PBS Parents (available at http://www.pbs.org/parents/education/going-to-school/supporting-your-learner/role-of-parents): Provides 11 tips for parents to act as role models for their children.

**How support systems impact adult careers.** Adults who have adequate support systems usually are aware of their needs. Countless CEOs of companies who recognize their weaknesses in organizational skills have assistants to monitor details and schedules. Some adults rely on external support, like career or life coaches, therapists, or medication to help them manage deficit areas. Families, friends, or business associates can also provide support.

Adults who don't have support systems are left to their own devices to find a career and may end up being underemployed—working in a job that is beneath their skill level. For example, a person who studies for a career in a competitive field like advertising but who is not highly motivated to utilize support systems may not be able to land a job in such a demanding career.

**Example of someone who lacked support.** Seelan Paramanandam Manickam is a musician who was diagnosed with ADHD in middle school when a guidance counselor and the school nurse told him he was hyperactive (Corman & Hallowell, 2006). However, his parents, both immigrants from Sri Lanka and very hard workers, did not accept that Manickam could have a disorder. They continued to believe he could control his behavior and had no patience for his difficulties, often punishing him harshly. Many parents, like Manickam's, are well-intentioned but don't take or have the time to learn about ADHD and how it impacts their children. Figure 20 details how Manickam built his support system.

## Productive Use of Technology
## (Primarily for Older Students)

**Background information.** Technology has made life easier for parents in many ways—instant access to information, the ability to keep track of where our children are, effective learning tools, and ease of communication. On the other hand, technology has created a source of huge power struggles and angst for parents as they try to control and monitor their children's consumption of media and use of social networking. If you are the parents of a tech-savvy teen, you know that struggle is very real. We want to encourage you to take the time to do as much as you can to ensure your child uses technology to her benefit and not to her detriment.

We see many children who are more or less addicted to video gaming, spending hours every day playing games. The saying, "Everything in moderation," would apply here. The important thing to remember is that while your child is spending time gaming, there are probably many more developmental tasks that are not being addressed. Helping your child strive for a balanced life with opportunities for physical activity, face-to-face social interaction, academic pursuits, family time, and chores is important. If your child is spending 15–20 hours on video games per week, something else has got to be falling by the wayside. Unfortunately, children with ADHD are often drawn to computer games because of the frequent and immediate rewards provided and the fast-changing images on the screen. If children are not feeling successful in their school and social lives, video games provide an alternate reality. Although video games can provide relaxation, learning opportunities, planning, and interaction with others online, they can also expose kids to a level of violence they are not capable of handling emotionally. As a parent, it is important to make these decisions your-

| Who | Seelan Paramanandam Manickam, Musician |
|---|---|
| **Natural Talents** | Musical |
| **Factor(s) That Needed Strengthening** | A more supportive setting at home: Fortunately, Manickam's teachers recognized his intelligence and musical talent and nurtured those talents. |
| **Key(s) to Success** | Manickam found and developed his musical passion for playing the trumpet. His parents allowed him to work with his sister's music teacher, who encouraged and helped him to find a way to go to college on scholarship to study music, even when his parents were opposed. Manickam recalled that the good teachers in high school "helped him find ways to work hard at things he didn't do well and did not make him feel like a failure in the process" (p. 84). However, he did not have the skills to manage college and started missing classes and assignments. He lost his scholarship, but his parents agreed to pay his tuition. College was a struggle, but he graduated. He realized he would need a graduate degree for his career but "was plagued with worries about failure, and he still had problems meeting deadlines and following through, especially with written work. After he took a summer off to mountain bike and think, Seelan grew up a bit. . . . Ready to learn the skills he would need to succeed, he finally took some classes that gave him tools he needed to get his act together" (p. 88). |
| **Advice** | Follow your passions and never give up on your gifts. |

*Figure 20.* Seelan Paramanandam Manickam and support systems (Corman & Hallowell, 2006).

self and not be goaded into allowing games that your gut instinct says are not right for your child because "everyone else is playing them."

Additionally, an estimated 25% of people with ADHD are addicted to the Internet, running a much higher risk of addiction than neurotypicals (Kutscher & Rosin, 2015, p. 22). The impulsivity associated with ADHD and acting before considering the consequences of the action can also result in children accepting friend requests from people they don't know, "sexting," and other inappropriate Internet use, which can significantly impact their lives for years to come.

The American Academy of Pediatrics issued revised guidelines for media consumption in 2018. Its recommendations for children include:

- **18 months and younger:** Avoid use of screen media other than video-chatting, such as Skype or FaceTime.
- **18–24 months:** Choose developmentally appropriate programming and view it with your child to help him understand and apply what he is seeing.
- **2–5 years:** Limit screen time to one hour a day and view media with your child.
- **6 years and up:** Have consistent limits on media and ensure it does not impinge on time for other activities.

Furthermore, the American Academy of Pediatrics recommended having media-free times together and media-free locations, such as bedrooms, as well as ongoing discussions about media safety and appropriate use.

On a positive note, technology used properly can help a student with disorganization, forgetfulness, and a weak sense of time become much more productive. Apps and programs abound to help with time management, focus, organization, information management, productivity, and academic subjects. Technology changes so quickly that we have provided only a few tools currently available that might be of help to your child. Stay abreast of changes to find technology that fits you and your family's needs.

**How unproductive use of technology may appear.** A child who is not using technology productively does not use it to help manage assignments, responsibilities, or promote learning. A child who doesn't use some technological advancements to help offset deficits will often miss deadlines, need constant nagging from others about responsibilities, and may fail at tasks in which she could have been successful.

**Strategies for strengthening productive use of technology.** As parents, we believe it is very important to monitor your child's technology use because of all of the significant risks out there, from posting inappropriate material, to cyberbullying, to identity theft, to exploitation. Many parents prefer to have computers in common areas of the house where it is easy to walk by and see what is on the screen at any time. Many parents insist on knowing their children's passwords and logins and spot check from time to time.

Some of the most effective and frequently used parental monitoring apps include Kidgy (available at https://kidgy.com), which is a parental control tool that allows users to regulate application usage and block apps that might promote harmful behavior. You can check on your children using the GPS tracking feature. It also includes a panic button, which your child can use in case of danger. Some call it a low-cost cyber nanny. Kids Zone Parental Controls for Android, Parental Control and Kid Tracker, and Qustodio are other good parental control apps that allow you to create a profile for your children and add apps that are appropriate for them. You can block unwanted text messages and prevent children from installing apps that you have not approved or making purchases on their own. MSpy (https://www.mspy.com) allows parents to monitor Internet browsing, searches, and texting. It enables parents to block people and has a location-tracking feature.

Table 24 is a list of additional strategies for improving your child's productive use of technology.

**Additional resources.** Books for children include:

- *Unplugged: Ella Gets Her Family Back* by Laura Pedersen (ages 5–8)
- *Doug Unplugged* by Dan Yaccarino (ages 5–9)

A useful online resource is TRUCE (available at http://www.truceteachers.org), which stands for Teachers Resisting Unhealthy Children's Entertainment and aims to help parents deal with the harmful impact of media on children's play, behavior, and school success.

**How use of technology appears in adult careers.** Adults who understand their needs can use technology to bridge weaknesses in their skill set and maximize their capabilities.

# Keys to Success

*Table 24*

Strategies for Strengthening Your Child's Productive Use of Technology

| Characteristics | Activities to Strengthen Productive Use of Technology |
| --- | --- |
| Does not awaken on his own in the morning | 1. Children as young as 8 can start to be responsible for getting themselves up. There are many interesting alarm clocks out there to help with the job. If your older child has a smartphone, have him get in the habit of setting the alarm feature on the clock icon. Even if a child has a smartphone, some parents prefer the use of an alarm clock. Some sound sleepers may need both. Place the alarms far enough away from the bed that the child has to get up to turn them off. |
| Does not use technology effectively to monitor due dates and activities | 1. Promote using a family calendar, such as Cozi Family Organizer, which allows calendar sharing and list creation, or Google Calendar.<br>2. Use task management apps in which you can create and manage to-do lists. The Homework App is an assignment tracker and planner available from the App Store. |
| Does not use technology to track school grades and assignments | 1. Use apps like the myHomework Student Planner (free with ads or $4.99 per year for premium) at https://myhomeworkapp.com or Class Manager-My Homework App available through Apple.<br>2. Make sure you and your child check any school websites that list grades and information from the teacher. |
| Does not use technology effectively to enhance learning | 1. Use YouTube videos or Kahn Academy to provide tutorials on skills.<br>2. Use Quizlet to prepare flash digital cards or use sets already created by teachers or students. It also allows games with study material.<br>3. Evernote (Evernote) or OneNote (Microsoft), both with free versions, let students create different digital notebooks for each class with links to helpful websites. Notability (Ginger Labs) has a recording feature that automatically syncs to handwritten or typed text. OneNote and Notability enable multiple color highlighting.<br>4. Ebooks make reading more enjoyable for some students. Audiobooks available at audible.com or iBooks sync with the electronic text and highlight each word as it is read.<br>5. Some students are able to use speech recognition software or Dictation on the Mac to help with writing assignments.<br>6. Earbuds help some students concentrate more effectively by blocking out distractions. |

Adults who don't make use of technology often miss deadlines, have difficulty keeping up with schedules, and miss opportunities for advancement.

**Example of someone whose life has been enhanced by effective use of technology.** Daniel Koh is the former Chief of Staff to the Mayor of Boston, MA. He was diagnosed with ADHD at age 14 (Reynolds, 2017). Figure 21 details how Koh uses technology productively.

## CONSIDER THIS

Nakia is a 14-year-old girl who has been diagnosed with ADHD and is suspected of having a learning disability in reading and written language. She currently has a 504 plan that provides accommodations, including cueing to stay on task, permissible movement in the classroom, and preferential seating. She likes school only for socializing and does not feel she is making progress in her academics. Her parents expect her to make the honor roll but are worried that she has lost her motivation for academic improvement. Teachers are concerned that she does not complete her classwork, does not do or forgets to turn in homework, and is more interested in socializing and being popular than working.

On the Multiple Intelligences Profile (see Figure 22), her natural strengths were in musical (20), interpersonal (18), and naturalistic intelligence (18). She loves music of all kinds, sings in the school choir, and is learning to play the guitar. She is very personable and can talk easily with peers or adults. She is keenly interested in nature and the environment. On the Keys to Success Survey (see Figure 23), her weakest areas, which could keep her from using her strengths, were in effective use of technology (4), motivation (9), and use of support systems (10).

A review of her assessments in reading showed Nakia had made no gains during the school year. Her parents called for a meeting with the district reading specialist, principal, ESE coordinator, and her teachers in attendance. The reading specialist recommended a specific intensive reading program available at the school. This pullout program

| Who | Daniel Koh, Politician |
|---|---|
| **Natural Talents** | Interpersonal, Logical, and Linguistic |
| **Factor(s) That Needed Strengthening** | Productive use of technology: Koh believes that spending time to keep an organized inbox is important and something he tends to daily. "I put my work inbox at zero at the end of every day," he said in an interview with U.S. News (para. 15). "Additionally, he does the same with his personal email inbox every Sunday night, explaining that these habits reduce clutter and allow him to start the day ahead with a more focused, organized approach." |
| **Key(s) to Success** | Following a strict schedule and effective use of technology are keys for Koh. He includes time for self-care, like going to the gym. He reported that he "uses Wunderlist, a cloud-based app that he says allows him to add items to a list, which is then accessible by both phone and computer"(para. 13). |
| **Advice** | Although there are bound to be circumstances that throw off any successful person's agenda on occasion, Koh says he's learned to let it roll off his back. "You learn to let some things go," he says. "If something doesn't work perfectly, it's OK. I try to stick as closely to my schedule as I can and maintain my positive habits" (para. 16). |

*Figure 21.* Daniel Koh and productive use of technology (Reynolds, 2017).

could be considered an intensive intervention as part of the Response to Intervention tier system, which could lead to Nakia's identification as a student with learning disabilities if the interventions are not successful.

To address her needs, her parents committed to:
1. monitoring homework nightly and implementing consequences involving loss of privileges when assignments were missed;
2. encouraging daily reading and having her transition to reading on an iPad, which enabled her to quickly access the meanings of unfamiliar words;

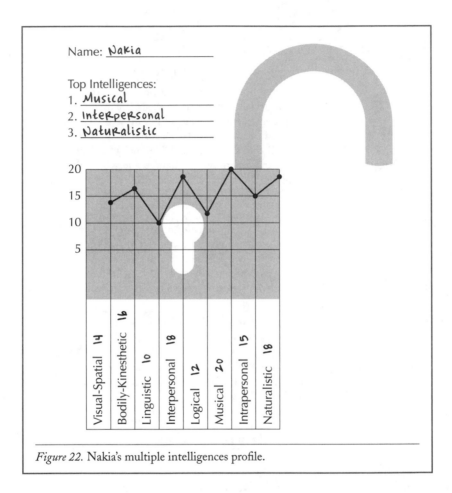

*Figure 22.* Nakia's multiple intelligences profile.

3. helping her develop an organizational system for her backpack so papers to be turned in at school were more accessible;
4. assisting her in developing a habit of monitoring her school grades on the computer;
5. working with her to improve her keyboarding skills to make doing homework more efficient, using many of the free programs available online, such as KidzType and Free Typing Game;
6. modifying their expectations to be in line with Nakia's capabilities;

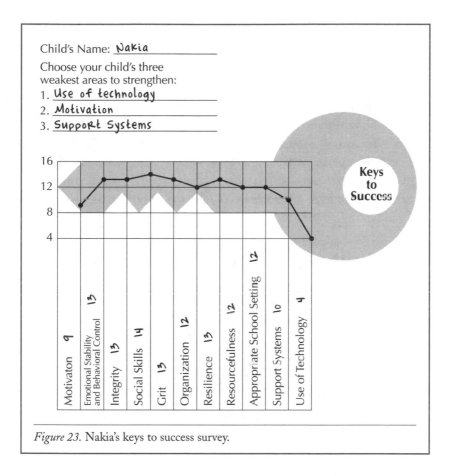

*Figure 23.* Nakia's keys to success survey.

7. agreeing to stay in close communication with teachers about her progress in her additional reading program; and
8. providing outside tutoring to bolster her reading skills.

Nakia's teachers committed to:

1. helping her set a small weekly goal to work toward;
2. assisting her in locating books on her reading level and in her areas of interest (music and nature);
3. seating her by an organized peer, who helped her remember to turn in homework;

4. letting her teach a short lesson to the class in science on a topic of her choice when she has been consistently turning in homework;
5. putting her strong social skills to work in teaching a concept she has mastered to another student;
6. noticing when she pays attention and commending her for it;
7. becoming more mindful of the number of negative comments directed at Nakia and trying to have many more positive than negative comments; and
8. praising her efforts more than the results.

# Take Away From This Chapter

In this chapter, you have been introduced to people from all walks of life who met with success in their lives. Our experience and research have shown that successful people with ADHD often accept the difficulties that may come with their ADHD and manage to work around them—but definitely have their ups and downs. Like everyone else, they have strengths and weaknesses but have managed to persevere and find great satisfaction in their lives. We sincerely wish the very same for your child.

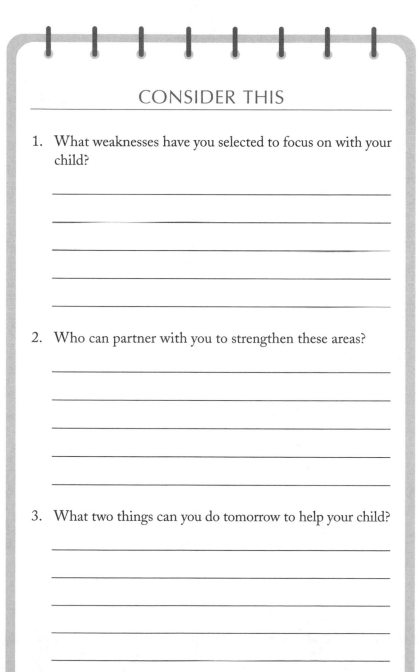

## CONSIDER THIS

1. What weaknesses have you selected to focus on with your child?

   _____

   _____

   _____

   _____

   _____

2. Who can partner with you to strengthen these areas?

   _____

   _____

   _____

   _____

   _____

3. What two things can you do tomorrow to help your child?

   _____

   _____

   _____

   _____

   _____

# Chapter 5

# Treatments for Success

Your life does not get better by chance, it gets better by change.
—Jim Robb

Treatment options for children with ADHD are a widely debated area. In this chapter, you will read about some of the research and options, as well as our professional opinion. Yet, ultimately, your treatment decision must include your beliefs, your interpretation of the research, consultation with professionals, and the cooperation of your child.

For most people, ADHD is a lifelong condition and requires vigilance about treatment. A longitudinal research study from Barkley and Fischer (2018) followed up on a number of lifestyle and health factors, such as tobacco and alcohol use, of people who had been diagnosed with ADHD Combined Type as children in the late 1970s. Utilizing an estimated life expectancy calculator and taking into consideration risk factors, Barkley and Fischer suggested that those individuals had a 9.5-year reduction in healthy estimated life expectancy (i.e., number of healthy years of life), and an 8.4-year reduction in total estimated life expectancy relative to a control sample without ADHD. Those individuals who had ADHD that persisted into adulthood had a 12.7-year reduction in estimated life expectancy. Factors that contributed to a person's lower estimated life expectancy included behavioral disinhibition (high impulsivity), which could be related to alcohol and drug use and smoking; lower verbal IQ; and hostility (anger). These results certainly support treating your child's ADHD.

# Multimodal Treatment of ADHD

The Multimodal Treatment of ADHD study (Multimodal Treatment Study of Children with ADHD Cooperative Group, 1999) was the largest national study of ADHD treatments, which included 579 children ages 7–9, who were diagnosed with ADHD Combined Type. The children with ADHD were randomly assigned to one of four treatment modes:
1. medication treatment alone,
2. intensive behavior therapy alone,
3. medication treatment combined with behavior therapy, or
4. community care in which parents selected their own treatment type.

After 14 months, results indicated that children receiving carefully monitored medication treatment or medication treatment plus intensive behavior therapy had lower levels of ADHD symptoms compared to those receiving intensive behavioral treatment alone or regular community care. This study did not suggest that medication is right for every child. During the study, all children improved in each of the four treatments. The study supported that children who took medication alone or medication with behavior therapy showed the greatest improvement. Of particular interest was that the results of the study showed that higher and more consistent stimulant dosages decreased the speed with which children grew. The reduced growth was in the range of 1 to 2 cm, but the effects diminished by the third year of treatment.

# ADHD Medication

The American Academy of Pediatrics (Subcommittee on Attention-Deficit/Hyperactivity Disorder, Steering Committee on Quality Improvement and Management, 2011) recommended medication as a frontline treatment approach to treating ADHD. This is because stimulant medication is the most widely used treatment for ADHD, as it has higher response rates than other interventions (Purdie, Hattie, & Carroll, 2002). Because we are not medical doctors, we encourage you to discuss your specific circumstances with your child's physician. The information we provide is based on research literature and our experiences working with families.

Here are four questions to consider when deciding if medication is right for your child:

1. How does my child's behavior/moodiness affect our home life?
2. How is my child performing in school?
3. How does my child feel about him- or herself?
4. How severe are my child's ADHD symptoms?

These four questions can help you consider if and why medication may help your child. In addition to reducing the core ADHD symptoms, medication may improve academic performance, behavior, and relationships with family and peers. Ingrid's son was 6 when he started medication. She made the decision to start medication because his behavior was getting him in trouble in kindergarten, he was falling behind in his learning, and home life was stressful. She asked herself, "Six is so young; should I put my son on medication?" After discussing her concerns with the pediatrician, she knew it was the right decision to help her son.

The large-scale research indicates ADHD medication helps decrease symptoms in 80% of children (Purdie et al., 2002). So out of 10 children, eight experience benefit, but two children do not. You won't know if medication will help your child unless you try it. Because ADHD occurs from mild to severe, medication may be less essential if your child is on the mild side. If you don't know if your child's ADHD is mild, moderate, or severe, ask the doctor or psychologist who diagnosed or is helping treat your child.

South Florida board-certified developmental and behavioral pediatrician Judith Aronson-Ramos, MD, provides medical treatment for pediatric patients (birth–18 years) with challenges in learning, behavior, development, and social-emotional functioning. She offers the following advice.

# Medications for ADHD

*By Judith Aronson-Ramos, MD*

Using medication for ADHD is often confusing and anxiety-provoking for parents. In considering the usage of medication for ADHD, there are many things to consider. First and foremost, it is always a partnership between parents, the child, and the physician, or the patient and the physician for older teens and young adults. In my practice, I address these concerns and work to develop a plan that is effective and acceptable to everyone involved. To make the best decision for yourself or your child, you need to be informed and consider all of your treatment options.

Once a decision to try medication had been made, there are a series of issues to discuss and consider in choosing the right medication for each individual. It is important to have an overview of all of the medications available. There are more than 25 FDA-approved medications for ADHD at this time. In general, we divide medications into two classes: stimulants and nonstimulants. This can be confusing to families—when you hear the word *stimulant* you think of a medication as stimulating your child who may actually need to calm down, focus, and be more in control. However, the term *stimulant* is a misnomer, as these medications actually calm and reduce hyperactivity. The following is a list of the FDA-approved medications generally used to treat ADHD symptoms in children and teens.

Methylphenidate:
- Methylphenidate (generic)
- Ritalin
- Ritalin LA
- Ritalin SR
- Methylin
- Methylin chewable
- Methylin liquid

- Methylin ER
- Metadate CD
- Metadate ER
- Concerta
- Focalin XR
- Focalin
- Daytrana (patch)

Amphetamine:
- Dextroamphetamine Sulfate (generic)
- Adderall

- Adderall XR
- Vyvanse

Nonstimulants:
- Strattera
- Intuniv

- Kapvay

## Key Questions About ADHD Medication

**Q: What do ADHD medications actually do to the body?**

**A:** ADHD medications increase *dopamine* in the brain by a variety of mechanisms. Some medications also increase *norepinephrine* but to a lesser degree. Both of these neurotransmitters occur naturally in the brain; the medications increase the naturally occurring substances.

**Q: How do doctors decide which medication to use?**

**A:** There are several factors to consider, including:
- mode of administration (i.e., pill, patch, liquid, or chewable);
- how long the medication needs to work (i.e., 4, 6, 8, 10, or 12 hours);
- underlying problems (e.g., insomnia, under- or overweight, etc.);

- family history (i.e., what has worked with other affected family members);
- age of the patient (effects can vary in younger vs. older children);
- cost and insurance coverage;
- interaction with other medications; and
- presence or absence of coexisting problems, such as motor tics, anxiety, or moodiness.

**Q: How do you know when a child is on the right medication?**

**A:** There are several ways to determine if a medication is working, such as:
- tracking symptom improvement with rating scales from parents, teachers, and others;
- self-reporting effects;
- if symptom reduction is notable in school, work, home, and play; and
- if the balance of positive effects and side effects is optimal.

**Q: What if the medications don't work?**

**A:** Thirty percent of the time, the first medication trialed works. Often, however, other medications need to be tried. Eighty percent of the time an effective medication or combination of medications can be found. Beyond medication trials, behavioral approaches need to be consistent. If there are truly no effects after an adequate medication trial, the diagnosis needs to be considered. In older individuals, physicians need to be certain there is no concomitant substance abuse.

**Q: How long will my child have to use medication?**

**A:** Length of treatment is individualized and based on needs. Hyperactivity decreases with age; however, demands on organizational skills increase with age. Some children no longer need medication during various points in their school years. Doctors and parents can work with older teens and young adults to try to reduce their need for medication through self-control, exercise, nutrition, supplements, coaching, and other strategies. Medication is always on a trial basis and should be started and stopped based on effectiveness. A medication trial is only a "trial," and fear of being on medication for life should not influence the decision to start medication.

**Q: What if there are bad side effects from medication?**

**A:** If a medication trial is successful, nearly all side effects can be managed. Many children will experience some reduction in appetite, difficulty falling asleep, and mood changes with stimulants. These side effects may improve on their own with time or be effectively managed with a variety of strategies (adding calories, taking melatonin, etc.). Nonstimulants have their own side effects depending on the medication. These side effects can include sedation (Kapvay, Intuniv), moodiness, and nausea (Strattera). Over time, many of these effects disappear. If not, there are specific ways to manage the side effects (e.g., taking nonstimulants at night, taking Strattera with food, etc.).

**Q: Will my child become a zombie?**

**A:** Affect and personality change, if they occur, are considered negative side effects and should be managed through medication changes. No child should continue on a medication that has a negative effect on his or her personality.

**Q: What if my teenager does not want to take the medication?**

**A:** Your child's physician needs a willing partner in medication trials and can assist with working through any resistance that arises. No child, however, should feel he or she is being forced to take medication.

**Q: Will medication teach my child the wrong lesson about drugs?**

**A:** On the contrary, untreated ADHD often leads to impulsivity and poor decision making, which can lead to substance abuse. Physicians rarely prescribe medication alone. Psychosocial treatments include parenting, organizational skills, and behavior plans to help with symptoms.

**Q: When will my child stop taking the medications?**

**A:** Discontinuation trials will be planned and monitored as you or your child see fit. Typically, a patient should be close to symptom-free before even considering this option. If there are still significant difficulties but adherence to medication is no longer desired or possible, there should be a plan to monitor symptoms and strategies to manage ongoing problems.

**Q: What do long-term studies show?**

**A:** Long-term studies show that there is no harm to the brain from use of ADHD medications. There are improvements in relationships and psychosocial functioning. ADHD symptoms persist over time, and although medication may not always be necessary, the problems that arise from ADHD need to be continuously worked on through a wide range of methods (coaching, organizational skills, outlets for activity, etc.). There are inconclusive effects on growth, with a small decrease in height cited as a potential concern. ADHD medications have been shown to protect teens from substance abuse. Medications can also reduce potential harm from accidents in driving, reckless behavior, or poor decision making.

---

The following information is written by board-certified child, adolescent, and adult psychiatrist, Michelle Chaney, MD, MScPH. She provides a quick read on current and emerging medications for ADHD. Chaney is currently on the staff at Florida Atlantic University's Counseling and Psychological Services in Boca Raton and Jupiter, FL. She is also a nonclinical faculty member at Massachusetts General Hospital in Boston, MA.

# Current and Emerging Medications for ADHD

*By Michelle Chaney, MD*

**Q: What are some of the latest advances in diagnosing ADHD?**

**A:** Although there is significant ongoing research about ADHD and many discoveries about its neurological causes, these findings have not changed standard diagnostic practices in recent years. Unfortunately, a single definitive brain scan or blood test to assist with the diagnosis of ADHD does not exist in clinical practice, at least not yet. There are a number of studies proving genetic links, as well as ongoing neuroimaging research across the life cycle. These findings may one day help us to better understand differences in ADHD presentation and enable more effective individualized treatment planning.

ADHD currently remains a clinical diagnosis that requires thoughtful evaluation by a skilled practitioner. Typically, this evaluation will include an extensive diagnostic interview and may incorporate rating scales, often completed by the child's parents and teachers. Psychological testing can be important to better understand emotional and cognitive functioning as well as possible learning disorders.

**Q: What are some of the most recent medications to come on the market?**

**A:** The most recent medications to come on the market for ADHD are variations of existing stimulant treatments. Stimulants enhance nerve-to-nerve communication to ultimately decrease hyperactivity and improve inattention symptoms. The newest preparations of stimulants come in different delivery systems to try to make taking the medication easier. For example, oral disintegrating tablets and liquids may be easier for children who have difficulty swallowing pills. Newer stimulant formulations have also been developed to last for various amounts of time, with extended release options typically providing symptom coverage for the entire day.

One of the newest medications approved by the FDA in 2018 is a methylphenidate called Jornay PM (was known as HLD200). It is taken before bed and has a special delivery technology to delay the medication release until the early morning. This is advertised to be particularly helpful for children who struggle with their early morning routine before school.

The biggest side effects of all stimulants are typically decreased appetite, insomnia, headaches, and upset stomach. Irritability, sadness, as well as worsening of ADHD symptoms when the medication wears off can also appear, but with much less frequency. It is reasonable for your physician to consider obtaining an electrocardiogram (EKG) before stimulant use depending on family history or presence of any cardiac defects; however, routinely obtaining an EKG is not considered mandatory.

Nonstimulant medications are often excellent choices for individuals who may not respond to stimulant medications or are intolerant to the adverse effects of stimulants. In addition, they may be first-choice options for individuals who have anxiety, tics, substance abuse, or depression. The antihypertensive agents may cause drowsiness; this can be helpful for some individuals with sleep difficulties. Side effects for Strattera include GI distress, sedation, decreased appetite, irritability, and, in rare circumstances, liver problems.

One of the additional areas of research for ADHD treatment involves the use of nicotinic receptors; nothing yet has come to market. In addition, a novel dual-acting dopamine and norepinephrine reuptake inhibitor medication is in development. This has not obtained FDA approval.

# Behavioral and Therapeutic Treatments

There are numerous treatments to use in conjunction with medication or in place of medication, but it can be overwhelming to know which treatment is the best one to use. Parents must consider cost, overall program effectiveness, and how long it may take for the treatment to work. Hodgson, Hutchinson, and Denson (2012) reviewed non-pharmacological (nonmedication) treatments for ADHD. There were 382 participants in 14 separate studies who received nonmedication-based psychological interventions to treat ADHD. Hodgson and colleagues reviewed studies evaluating behavior modification, neurofeedback therapy, multimodal psychosocial treatment, school-based programs, working memory training, parent training, and self-monitoring treatments. Of these treatments, the two with the most commonly reported improvement were neurofeedback and behavior modification. The researchers used a statistical procedure to measure effect size of treatments, and the largest improvement was using neurofeedback. The researchers determined that, overall, the psychological treatments for ADHD were more effective with girls. Children with ADHD Combined Type benefited the least from psychological treatments.

Sonuga-Barke and colleagues (2013) conducted a metanalysis on 54 nonmedication interventions for dietary and psychological treatments of ADHD. They concluded that free fatty acid supplementation and excluding artificial food color allayed ADHD symptoms, "although the effect of the former are small and those of the latter may be limited to ADHD patients with food sensitivities" (p. 285). There was moderate support for behavioral interventions, neurofeedback, and cognitive training. However, the researchers noted additional studies are needed to document their effectiveness before they can be supported as high-success ADHD treatments.

In our work, behavior therapy is one treatment that has helped many of our clients. If your child's behavior is out of control and you are at your wit's end, then consider behavior therapy. The goal of behavior therapy is to change your child's behavior by changing how she responds to the physical or social environment. You can learn specific techniques to increase your skill in modifying your child's behavior, while teaching your child to regulate her own behavior. According to the Centers for Disease Control and Prevention (2018), through behavior therapy, parents learn how to:

- Strengthen the relationship with their child through positive communication, for example, active listening and describing emotions
- Reinforce good behavior, for example, giving positive attention and effective praise for good behavior
- Create structure and provide consistent discipline, for example, giving effective instructions, withholding attention for unwanted behavior, and effective use of time-out (para. 9)

The following parent training included with the behavior therapy programs help improve behavior in young children with ADHD. These are evidenced-based, which means independent research studies have documented that these programs help improve behavior.

- **Triple P Parenting:** This is a program to prevent and treat behavioral and emotional problems in children and teens.
- **Incredible Years Parenting Program:** This is a proactive and preventative program that helps parents and teachers treat behavior and emotional problems in children from birth through age 12.
- **Parent-Child Interaction Therapy:** This is a program in which parents are coached by a therapist who is watching them and their child interact.
- **New Forest Parenting Programme:** This program is based in the United Kingdom and helps children between the ages of 3 and 11 with moderate to severe ADHD. The program takes place in the family's home.
- **Community Parent Education Program:** This program was developed in Canada to help parents of children ages 3–5 become proactive and preventative in improving interactions and reducing undesirable behavior.

Most pediatricians have a list of professionals in the area that provide parent training in behavior therapy. In addition, your insurance company may have a list of approved providers. You may also find providers through websites such as CHADD (https://chadd.org) or ADDitude (https://www.additudemag.com).

# Neurofeedback

Neurofeedback is a nonmedication supplemental approach for treating ADHD. It is challenging to pinpoint a concise definition of neurofeedback. For instance, the International Society for Neurofeedback and Research (2010) has a five-paragraph explanation on its website under the heading, "Definition of Neurofeedback." In basic terms, our brain produces measurable electrical signals or brainwaves. In children with ADHD, the brainwaves may be going too fast, which contributes to hyperactivity and impulsivity, or they may be going too slow, which contributes to inattention. Neurofeedback measures electrical waves with a device called an electroencephalograph (EEG). The purpose of neurofeedback is to help a person understand his or her brain and therefore change his or her behavior.

There are home-based and clinic-based neurofeedback treatment systems, and each has its pros and cons. The home-based neurofeedback systems are initially more expensive because you are purchasing equipment, whereas the clinic-based systems are often a pay-as-you-go approach but cost more overall. Some clinics offer a discount if you purchase packages of sessions; usually 20–30 sessions are recommended. The home-based neurofeedback systems offer the convenience of having no travel time, but some children do not work well with their parents. A benefit of a clinic-based neurofeedback program is the personalized clinical experience and support you receive in helping hone the treatment to maximize your child's benefits.

Before you invest money into treatment, a primary question to answer is, "Does neurofeedback work?" The research on neurofeedback as a treatment for ADHD is mixed. Lofthouse, Arnold, Hersch, Hurt, and DeBeus (2012) reviewed 14 neurofeedback studies that included children from ages 5 to 15. They concluded that "neurofeedback treatment for pediatric ADHD can be currently considered as 'probably efficacious' and in need of a large multisite triple-blind sham-controlled randomized control study to settle the issue" (p. 369). Since that time, Cortese and colleagues (2016) conducted a meta-analysis review of neurofeedback treatment. They noted limitations to the study but overall concluded that "the current meta-analysis shows that evidence from well-controlled trials with probably blinded outcomes does not support neurofeedback as an effective treatment for ADHD" (p. 453).

Based on these studies and in our experiences working with families, we recommend you proceed with caution on this treatment, but if you have discretionary money and time, neurofeedback is a treatment worth considering.

# Mindfulness

Mindfulness is an increasingly popular nonmedication method to help children learn to control their bodies and brains. Kabat-Zinn (2003) defined mindfulness as "the awareness that emerges through paying attention on purpose, in the present moment, and nonjudgmentally to the unfolding of experience moment by moment" (p. 145). Many children with ADHD can learn how to purposely pay attention.

According to van der Oord, Bögles, and Peijnenburg (2012), through mindful parenting, parents learn to

(1) be deliberately and fully present in the here and now with their child in a non-judgmental way; (2) take care of themselves, as this is the basis for parenting; (3) accept difficulties of their child; and (4) answer rather than react to difficult behavior of their child. (p. 142)

The researchers found that parents noticed a reduction in their child's ADHD symptoms and their own ADHD symptoms after the training. However, teachers did not rate the children as having a significant reduction of ADHD-related behavior. The researchers inferred that positive interactions of practicing the mindfulness exercises together between the parent and child may have helped improve the overall relationship.

Mindfulness has also been used effectively to help children handle worry and anxiety because it helps children get in touch with and accept emotions without judgment. Mindfulness can also help parents increase their awareness of emotions that, in turn, help them to choose responses to their children more carefully and thoughtfully.

Actress Goldie Hawn developed a strong interest in helping children deal with stress and anxiety through mindfulness and meditation. Through the Hawn Foundation, she asked a team of educators, neurologists, psychologists, and social scientists to develop a curriculum that involves lessons on how the brain works and also incorporates social-emotional development and metacognition (thinking about thinking) through meditation (Wickelgren, 2011). The curriculum is called *MindUp*, and it is currently being successfully implemented in a number of schools.

# Food-Based Treatments

One of the emerging areas in the treatment of ADHD is medical food. The FDA designates medical food as "Generally Recognized as Safe," which means experts have recognized the food additives as safe. A medical food is made up of highly concentrated and purified natural ingredients. Medical foods are more than just a special food recommended by a physician as part of your child's overall diet. A medical food, as defined in section 5(b)(3) of the Orphan Drug Act (21 U.S.C. 360ee(b)(3)), is

> a food which is formulated to be consumed or administered enternally under the supervision of a physician and which is intended for the specific dietary management of a disease or condition for which distinctive nutritional requirements,

based on recognized scientific principles, are established by medical evaluation.

The patient should be under the supervision of a health care provider. Thus, you can get medical food via prescription or by a patient attestation, which is simply acknowledging you are under the supervision of your physician. The medical food can be labeled and marketed for management of a specific disease or condition. Medical food differs from supplements like fish oil, which you purchase at your neighborhood store. A supplement may not be labeled or marketed to address a particular disease or condition. Supplements are for maintaining health in individuals who are assumed healthy.

The company currently marketing heavily in the ADHD arena is VAYA Pharma with a product called Vayarin. According to VAYA Pharma's website, this product was designed to control the lipid imbalances associated with ADHD. The product includes omega-3 fish oil along with VAYA Pharma's proprietary ingredient, phosphatidylserine. In its clinical trial study, VAYA Pharma reported an improvement in the behavior of children with ADHD Hyperactive-Impulsive Type and those with emotional dysregulation (anger, aggression, behaviors). At the time of publication, many health insurance plans do not cover Vayarin, so it is a hefty out-of-pocket, monthly expense for parents.

Special diets have not been proven to have large-scale positive results for children with ADHD. On one hand, logic tells you that sugar makes a hyper kid even more hyper, but science does not support that. Once again we turn to our colleague Dr. Aronson-Ramos for her insights into special diets for ADHD.

---

# Special Diets for ADHD

*By Judith Aronson-Ramos, MD*

Presently, there isn't a single specialized diet documented to treat or improve the symptoms of ADHD. This is in spite of many different claims and anecdotal evidence to the contrary. The majority of specialized diets are elimination diets, which remove offending foods and additives from the diet. However, from the Feingold diet to casein- and gluten-free, among others, there is still no scientifically-sound evidence that any of these diets work. Still, many families want to do something to improve nutrition and hedge their bets on using dietary interventions, which may at least positively contribute to improving the symptoms of their child with ADHD.

We do know that some children are sensitive to dyes and preservatives, which may worsen hyperactivity and impulsivity. This is true more for younger children. Sugar has not been shown to be a factor in worsening ADHD. However, it only makes sense that eating poorly—a lot of junk food, refined carbohydrates, excessively processed foods, etc.—can't be good for you.

I recommend certain practices of healthy eating, which are not restrictive and may benefit the child or adolescent with ADHD. This includes the following principals:

1. **Eat clean, whole foods.** This means shopping the periphery of the grocery store more than the aisles. Eat fruits, vegetables, nuts, seeds, meat, fish, cheese, and yogurt (essentially real foods). For more on this topic, read *Food Rules* by Michael Pollan, and visit his website https://michaelpollan.com. He also has a page of links for families.

2. **Avoid preservatives, dyes, trans fats, high-fructose corn syrup, and additives when possible.** If you can eat organic, this may be preferable, although this has not been of proven benefit either. However, eating organic often eliminates many of the ingredients in processed foods you want to avoid, so it does simplify shopping.

3. **Include the "superfoods" in your diet.** These are foods that have well-documented health benefits, including improved immune function, enhanced neurological functioning, lowering cholesterol, and more. You can be creative in how these foods are served and prepared to get your children to eat them. They are good for parents, too. There is bound to be some-

thing on this list for everyone: beans, blueberries, broccoli, oats, oranges, pumpkin, salmon, soy, spinach, tea (green or black), tomatoes, turkey, walnuts, yogurt.

4. **Be sure your child is ingesting enough protein in the day, including breakfast and lunch.** Many children are protein-free throughout their day, eating mostly carbohydrates—bagels, waffles, and cereal for breakfast; pasta, pizza, and salad for lunch. These are low-protein meals. Encourage at least a small amount of protein—equivalent to the size of your child's fist—with all meals, especially breakfast and lunch. This means at breakfast including foods such as eggs, yogurt, nuts, high-protein cereals and breads, energy bars with protein, smoothies with protein powder, healthy breakfast meats (turkey sausage, bacon, etc.). Lunch ideally should have a protein source, such as a turkey sandwich, peanut butter and jelly on whole-grain bread, healthy lunch meats, tuna (sparingly), high-protein pasta, bean burritos, etc. It can be done! School-bought lunches are often a bust, unless you have a cafeteria offering healthy choices.

5. **Avoid sugary and caffeinated drinks.** These cause high peaks and troughs in insulin production and will impair concentration and focus.

6. **Use healthy fats.** These are nonhydrogenated, unsaturated, or polyunsaturated fats that don't clog arteries and, instead, lead to improved cerebrovascular (brain blood flow), as well as cardiovascular effects. Good fats include olive oil, canola oil, peanut oil, and corn oil. Bad fats include butter, coconut oil, palm oil, hydrogenated oils, and others. Research shows that certain fats, such as omega-3 fatty acids, reduce inflammation and may help lower the risk of certain chronic diseases. Omega-3 fatty acids are highly concentrated in the brain and are important for cognitive performance and behavioral function. Taking an omega-3 fatty acid supplement may be beneficial. To read more about fats and the role of omega-3 fatty acids in the diet, visit https://www.draronsonramos.com/wp-content/uploads/2017/02/Omega-3-Fatty-Acids-and-ADHD1.pdf.

7. Eating healthy does *not* have to be boring or a battle, especially with your teenager. The following books are specifically recommended for pre-teens and teens:
   - *Chew on This: Everything You Don't Want to Know About Fast Food* by Eric Schlosser and Charles Wilson
   - *The Omnivore's Dilemma: The Secretes Behind What You Can Eat* (Young Reader's Edition) by Michael Pollan

Useful documentaries include *Food Inc.*, *Super Size Me*, *Fast Food Nation*, *Forks Over Knives*, and *Fresh*. Watch them as a family. Additional online resources include Fizzy's Lunch Lab by PBS Kids for younger children (https://pbskids.org/lunchlab), and Girlshealth.gov (http://www.girlshealth.gov), and Fuel Up to Play 60 (https://www.fueluptoplay60.com) for adolescent girls and boys.

---

# ADHD Coaching and Video Coaching

ADHD coaching is a complementary and effective approach (Kubik, 2010; Merriman & Codding, 2008) for teaching real-life skills to people with ADHD. Coaching can be used with students from elementary school through college and into adulthood. Coaching works best when the student is an invested and active participant. Your child must be willing to engage, learn, and practice the new skills. Skills taught in coaching are often those that are weaker in those with ADHD, such as time management, goal setting, emotional regulation, problem solving, organization, self-monitoring, motivation, and self-talk. As you can tell from these topics, coaching is not tutoring, as coaches do not work on reading, math, and writing.

In order for coaching to be effective, several factors should be considered:
1. What are my expectations?
2. Does my child work best with a male or female?
3. Does my child have the willingness to learn?
4. Will my child work best in-person or via video?

5. Is the coach available in between sessions or only during our scheduled time?
6. Does the coach communicate with other professionals?
7. Will the coaching skills transfer to real life?

In our experience, coaching works when there is the right fit between your child and the coach. Coaching is more than imparting skills; it's about developing a relationship. Your child must like, respect, and trust the coach. A coach needs to be a combination of a teacher, mentor, and encourager. We find coaching also is most effective when you are working with an experienced coach. Thus, you should interview the coach to ask about his or her experience in helping kids with needs similar to your child. You want a coach with similar beliefs, so your child receives the same messages from both you and the coach. Your child would be conflicted if you believe grades are important, whereas your coach believes effort is the most important outcome.

*Coaching works best when the student is an invested and active participant.*

Because coaching is an expense and ADHD coaches are not in all geographic areas, you may consider coaching your own child if you have some expertise in the area. If you would like to coach your own child, there are some good guidebooks that you can use, such as:

- *Empowering Youth With ADHD: Your Guild to Coaching Adolescents and Young Adults for Coaches, Parents, and Professionals* by Jodi Sleeper-Triplett
- *Coaching Students With Executive Skills Deficits* by Peg Dawson and Richard Guare
- *Coaching College Students With Executive Function Problems* by Mary R. T. Kennedy

A growing number of ADHD specialists provide video-based coaching that bridges any geographical distances, reduces travel time, and opens up access to a larger number of coaches. The coaches use video technology to communicate with your child and may use screen-sharing features. The coaching process is similar; it involves goal setting, skill development, practice, and feedback. With video coaching, your child may be able to use his or her smart device to be coached as he or she is transported home from school, right after school is completed, while waiting on campus for sports or band practice, or in a number of nontraditional environments.

You can find ADHD coaches online or at these websites:

- ADHD Coaches Organization: https://www.adhdcoaches.org
- CHADD's Professional Directory: https://chadd.org/profess ional-directory
- ADD Coach Academy: https://addca.com

A program of CHADD through the National Resource Center on AD/HD provides information on complementary treatments and other interventions for ADHD at https://chadd.org/about-adhd/ complementary-and-other-interventions.

## CONSIDER THIS

1. What treatments have helped your child?

_____

_____

_____

_____

_____

2. Should you revisit starting or adding a treatment for your child?

_____

_____

_____

_____

_____

3. What types of treatments are available in your community?

_____

_____

_____

_____

_____

# Chapter 6

# Understanding Your Rights[1]

A word of encouragement from a teacher to a child can change a life. A word of encouragement from a spouse can save a marriage. A word of encouragement from a leader can inspire a person to reach her potential.

—John C. Maxwell

Even though you are striving hard to help your child with ADHD make the best of it, he or she may need additional support in school. If your child attends a public school and his or her ADHD significantly impacts his or her academic life, the following federal laws could enable him or her to receive some assistance if he or she qualifies:

- Section 504 of the Rehabilitation Act of 1973 (referred to as Section 504) and its companion federal laws—Americans with Disabilities Act of 1990 (ADA) and Americans with Disabilities Act Amendments Act of 2008 (ADAAA); and

---

1 Sections of this chapter are adapted with permission from *Raising Boys With ADHD: Secrets for Parenting Healthy, Happy Sons* by J. W. Forgan and M. A. Richey, 2012, Waco, TX: Prufrock Press.

- Individuals with Disabilities Educational Improvement Act of 2004 (called IDEA), which began as Public Law 94–142, the Education for All Handicapped Children Act in 1975, and has been amended multiple times.

The purpose of both of these laws is to see that the educational needs of students with disabilities are met so that they can progress in school to the best of their abilities. Section 504 can cover short-term problems like a broken arm or an illness, as well as a disability related to learning, behavior, or other health-related conditions, including ADHD if it significantly impacts education. Section 504 has a broader definition of disability than IDEA, so a child may qualify for a 504 plan but not be eligible under IDEA. Section 504 provides accommodations like extended time, frequent redirections, or a behavior plan. IDEA entitles the child to an Individualized Education Plan (IEP) and special education instruction, and the disability must fall within 13 categories, including Other Health Impaired, which is where ADHD is categorized. The other 12 categories are autism, deaf-blindness, deafness, emotional disturbance, hearing impairment, intellectual disability, multiple disabilities, orthopedic impairment, speech or language impairment, traumatic brain injury, and visual impairment.

*Sometimes the school will initiate the process for services and accommodations, but often parents need to take the leadership role.*

An important thing to know is that just having a disability does not automatically qualify your child for a 504 plan or an IEP. The school must determine that the disability impacts the child's ability to learn and progress. As with most things these days, there is a process. Get ready to delve into more complexity! Sometimes the school will initiate the process for services and accommodations, but often parents need to take the leadership role. Whether you take the lead or not, it is critical to document every conversation you have, noting the date, people present, and what was discussed. The school staff may be very well-intentioned, but they often have so many responsibilities that it is easy for requests to get lost. (As you read further, you will see two sample letters requesting consideration for a 504 plan and one for consideration for an IEP under IDEA.) Before proceeding, it is important to understand the parameters of both Section 504 and IDEA to assist in determining which best fits your child's needs. Remember, you are almost always going to be your child's best advocate.

# What Is Section 504?

Section 504 is a federal civil rights law that protects children ages 3–21 against discrimination in public and nonreligious schools, including colleges and technical schools receiving federal funds. However, it does not provide any funding; it simply mandates accommodations and some services, like small-group instruction. The intent is to provide a level playing field so the student's disability will not interfere with his or her access to education. Section 504 states:

> No qualified individual with a disability shall, on the basis of disability, be excluded from participation in or be denied the benefits of the services, programs or activities of a public entity, or be subjected to discrimination by any public entity. (35.130, Subpart B, p. 549)

According to ADA (1990),

The term "disability" means, with respect to an individual—
A.  has a physical or mental impairment that substantially limits one or more major life activities
B.  has a record of such impairment
C.  regarded as having such impairment. (HR 3195 RH)

The definition of "disability" was broadened under ADAAA (2008) to note that the disability must substantially limit one or more major life activities. Additional examples of major life activities included "learning, reading, concentrating, thinking, communicating, and working " (Section 2A). ADAAA clarified that an impairment could limit one major activity but not others and could be episodic. It further stated that the effects of medication and other devices for ameliorating the effects of the handicap should not be considered when determining if an impairment substantially limits a major activity. If your son is taking medication, the school team must consider his academic performance and behavior before he starts taking medication. The law specifies that a broad interpretation be given to the term "substantially limited."

Your child could meet items B or C in the ADA (1990) definition of "disability" and be guaranteed freedom from discrimination, but he would *not* be eligible for services and accommodations under a 504 plan *unless* he had met the first requirement of "a physical or mental impairment that substantially limits one or more major life activities." In essence, your child can be diagnosed with ADHD by an outside source or suspected of having ADHD but still not be determined eligible for a 504 plan because he or she demonstrates no substantial impairment in the school setting. A team of personnel from the school, which isn't tightly defined by 504 and doesn't always include parents, must determine if the ADHD "substantially limits" your child's access to an education on a case-by-case basis. However, because the law specifies that a broad interpretation be given to the term "substantially limited," you can advocate for your child and make sure the 504 team has a clear picture of your child and his or her struggles. Some parents bring advocates or attorneys to the table, but Mary Anne's experience as a school psychologist has shown that this is usually unnecessary. If you disagree with the team, there are several options, including mediation or, ultimately, a lawsuit.

# What Is IDEA?

IDEA is the federal law that states a free and appropriate education must be provided to all students who have a disability, meet their state's eligibility criteria, and have an *educational need* for special education services. IDEA provides funding for instruction, tailored to your child's unique needs, from a special education teacher, as well as related services like occupational therapy. As noted previously, Other Health Impaired (OHI) is the eligibility category most often considered for children with ADHD.

If a child is considered for services under the Other Health Impaired eligibility, he or she must have a diagnosis (such as ADHD), which significantly impacts his or her ability to learn and perform in the classroom to the extent that he or she would require special education services. Factors other than his or her test scores should be considered. Those factors might include "grades, homework completion, independent work habits, alertness, sleeping in class, class participation and attendance, ability to complete schoolwork and tests within specified time frames, relationships with peers, and compliance with rules" (Durheim & Zeigler Dendy, 2006, p. 128).

Federal law defines OHI as

having limited strength, vitality or alertness, including a heightened alertness to environmental stimuli, that results in limited alertness with respect to the educational environment, that:

A. Is due to chronic or acute health problems such as asthma, attention deficit disorder, or attention deficit hyperactivity disorders, diabetes, epilepsy, a heart condition, hemophilia, lead poisoning, leukemia, nephritis, rheumatic fever, and sickle cell anemia; and

B. Adversely affects a child's educational performance. (IDEA, 2004, Section 300.8(c)(9))

185

Your child could have a chronic health problem, like ADHD, as defined in item A but may *not* be determined to be eligible for services, accommodations, and modifications under IDEA unless his or her ADHD *substantially limits* his or her educational performance. Members of the IEP team under IDEA are specified by law and must include the parents, a teacher knowledgeable about the child, a special education teacher, an administrator (usually called a Local Education Authority or LEA, who is knowledgeable about the laws, disabilities, and general curriculum), and someone who can interpret test results, such as a school psychologist or speech and language pathologist. IDEA gives parents a range of ways to resolve disputes, which include mediation, filing a due process complaint, and all of the way up to filing a lawsuit.

# How Are 504 and IDEA Different?

Generally, children who qualify for IDEA are more impaired and require more services than those best served by a 504 plan. IDEA provides actual funding to schools for special education instruction specified in an IEP, while a 504 plan provides no additional funding to schools but affords your child accommodations and some services, such as a quiet place to work, use of educational aids such as computers, or small-group instruction. As you would expect, the qualification procedure is less stringent for Section 504. More students qualify for help under the 504 law.

IDEA requires the development of an IEP that specifies the student's current levels of performance, specific goals written for a year in all areas in which he or she is below grade-level peers (with specification about how these goals will be monitored), and details about where and for how long special education services will be provided. A 504 plan requires only written documentation of accommodations. Members who convene to write a 504 plan are not as clearly delineated as members of the IEP team are under IDEA (as outlined in the previous section). They should, however, be people who are familiar with the child and understand the evaluation and accommodations needed.

IDEA requires a formalized evaluation that might include a psychoeducational evaluation of the child's intelligence, academic levels, and processing abilities and possibly behavior rating scales. It could require a medical diagnosis of ADHD. Eligibility criteria can vary by school districts. 504 requires some documentation of the child's difficulties, but it doesn't have to be a diagnosis. It could include results of rating scales, teacher and parent information, as well as medical information.

IDEA requires consideration of reevaluation needs every 3 years. Many times, those reevaluations might be results of assessments and written observations provided by the classroom teacher. A 504 plan does not have a specific 3-year reevaluation component.

More specific parental rights come into play, such as clearly defined due process rights, when there is a serious disagreement between the school district and the parents over the need for an evaluation or determination of services. Section 504 provides for parent rights that are not as extensive as those under IDEA but still allow parents to contest a 504 determination.

Paperwork required in IDEA is more stringent, such as requiring specific written notice of eligibility or ineligibility. Under IDEA, an official IEP meeting is required before any change in placement can occur. The 504 requires no such meeting for a "significant change" in placement, but the parents must be notified. Table 25 further outlines the differences between the two laws.

# How Are 504 and IDEA Alike?

Both are based on federal laws that require that a child with a disability receive a free and appropriate public education (FAPE). As we've said earlier, the laws attempt to level the playing field, so your child will have the same access to education as nondisabled peers.

*Table 25*
How IDEA and Section 504 Differ

| IDEA | 504 |
|---|---|
| Office of Special Education of the U.S. Department of Education responsible for enforcement | Office for Civil Rights of the U.S. Department of Education responsible for enforcement |
| Students generally more impaired and require more service | Students generally don't require special instruction |
| Funding provided based on disability category | No funding provided to schools, but schools receiving IDEA funds must meet 504 requirements |
| More stringent qualification procedure | Less stringent qualification procedure |
| Individualized Education Plan (IEP) developed | 504 plan written |
| Members of IEP team specified by law | 504 team may vary by school district |
| Formal evaluation necessary | Some documentation of difficulties necessary |
| Reevaluation to be considered every 3 years | No reevaluation specified |
| More specific parental rights | Parent rights provided but not as stringent as IDEA |
| Official IEP meeting and parent permission required before change in placement can occur | No meeting required, but parent should be informed |

*Note.* From *Raising Boys With ADHD: Secrets for Parenting Healthy, Happy Sons* (p. 198), by J. W. Forgan and M. A. Richey, 2012, Waco, TX: Prufrock Press. Copyright 2012 by Prufrock Press. Reprinted with permission.

Both can provide accommodations, such as extended time to complete work, lessons broken down into smaller segments or "chunked," and copies of notes provided for the student's use.

Both require a formal eligibility process with paperwork that must be kept confidential. This allows the teacher and those working with the child to have knowledge of the disability and the required accommodations. Each plan requires an annual review, although parents can request a review at any time.

Both laws require that your child be educated in the least restrictive environment with nondisabled peers as much as possible. Both eligibilities transfer if your child moves to a different school but may have to be rewritten.

*The laws attempt to level the playing field, so your child will have the same access to education as nondisabled peers.*

Due process rights are provided by both laws when a parent disagrees with a school district over a child being eligible or provided services. The due process in IDEA is specified by federal law, whereas the due process in Section 504 is left up to the local school district. The similarities between IDEA and Section 504 are further summarized in Figure 24.

# What Determines Which Is Most Appropriate for My Child?

The decision will be made based on the needs of your child and the extent of his or her impairment. If your child needs individualized instruction from a special education teacher, an eligibility covered under IDEA should be considered. If your child is eligible for special education, the goal will be to have him or her remain in a general classroom as much as possible while still getting the help he or she needs. With eligibility under IDEA, he or she could also access other services as needed, such as counseling, occupational therapy, or language therapy. Children with ADHD may have more than one eligibility. For example, a comprehensive evaluation may determine that your child has a specific learning disability (SLD) in addition to ADHD, which would be labeled as Other Health Impaired (OHI).

How are IDEA and Section 504 alike?
- Both are federal laws requiring FAPE.
- Both have accommodations and some services available.
- A formal eligibility process is required for both.
- Paperwork for both laws must be kept confidential.
- Under both laws, the child is to be educated in the least restrictive environment with his nondisabled peers as much as possible.
- Eligibilities under both laws transfer from school to school but may have to be rewritten.
- Under both laws, due process rights are provided when a parent disagrees with the school district.

*Figure 24.* Similarities between IDEA and Section 504. From *Raising Boys With ADHD: Secrets for Parenting Healthy, Happy Sons* (p. 198), by J. W. Forgan and M. A. Richey, 2012, Waco, TX: Prufrock Press. Copyright 2012 by Prufrock Press. Reprinted with permission.

On the other hand, if your child is doing relatively well, he or she may only need accommodations in the classroom, such as being reminded to pay attention, permissible movement, or extended time, so his or her needs could be met through a 504 plan. Parents are required by law to be part of the decision-making process under IDEA and are generally included in 504 eligibility in most states.

## Navigating the Process to Consider Eligibility Under 504

Either you or the school initiates a meeting to discuss whether or not you child needs a 504 plan. Sometimes it may come up during a parent-teacher conference. If you are requesting the consideration, we recommend you put your request in writing to the 504 coordinator or the person handling 504 at your child's school. (See the sample letter included in this chapter requesting a 504.) If you do not hear back in a reasonable amount of time, say 10 school days, send a follow-up request. If you still do not get a response, contact the principal. In our experience, it is always advantageous to work with the school staff, but if they are stonewalling your request, you will have to appeal to a district-level 504 coordinator or an outside source. For the meeting and beyond:

1. Gather any documentation you may have, such as an ADHD diagnosis by a doctor or psychologist (not absolutely necessary but helpful), school records highlighting your child's difficulties (e.g., report cards or teacher conference notes), and interventions that have proven helpful to your child in the past (e.g., cue cards to help him or her remember a process like what to do for dismissal, preferential seating near the teacher, reminders to stay focused, help breaking his or her work down into small manageable chunks, etc.). The school should gather information about your child's classroom functioning, which might include teacher observations, grades, and results of standardized assessments.

2. If the school feels an evaluation is necessary, your consent will be required for anything that is not routinely done for all children. An evaluation could range from a full evaluation by the school psychologist, to rating scales, to testing done by the teacher. If the school is doing testing, the school has 60 school days from the time consent is signed to complete the testing.

3. Make sure a follow-up meeting is set.

4. If and when the team decides that your child's ADHD "substantially limits" his school performance or behavior, it would determine him to be eligible for a formal 504 plan. Then, work with the teacher and 504 coordinator to develop a 504 plan that will meet your child's needs. The 504 plan generally includes:
   - specific accommodations or services,
   - name(s) of those who will provide the services, and
   - name of the person responsible for seeing that the accommodations are followed.

Although a 504 plan includes strategies and assistance that an effective teacher would normally implement, it is always important to have it formalized and in writing. Without it, one year you may have a teacher who makes accommodations and the next year, one who does not. Going forward, you want to ensure your child has the needed accommodations provided consistently from classroom to classroom. Our experience has shown that it is better to focus on a few much-needed accommodations, rather than a lengthy list. Remember that the teacher has many other students, some of whom also have 504 plans or IEPs. We have found that a few important accommodations are more likely to be implemented daily than a laundry list of items, some of which may not be very important. Try to ensure that the accommodations are followed. If not, you will need to ask for another meeting. Generally, a review is done annually.

Kimberly Spire-Oh is a special education attorney representing students and their families across Florida. She also volunteers with local, state, and national organizations in trying to improve public policy relating to education and disabilities. She provided the following information about 504 and wrote a sample letter that you can utilize as you request services for your child with ADHD.

---

# Information and Sample Letter Requesting Consideration of 504 Plan

*By Kimberly Spire-Oh*

Not all students who receive diagnoses of ADHD or other conditions find that their symptoms affect their success in school. However, in many cases, ADHD negatively impacts a student academically, behaviorally, socially, or with regard to independent functioning, and all of these skill sets are considered essential parts of a student's education. In those situations, a 504 plan can allow the student to fully access the curriculum and programs offered by the school by providing for reasonable accommodations and related services that help address the ADHD symptoms.

In order to get a 504 plan, a student must provide documentation from a medical doctor that lists the student's diagnosis of ADHD and type (as well as any other relevant conditions), describes how the condition(s) affect(s) the student, and makes suggestions for possible accommodations or services that would help the student succeed in school. Whether the diagnosis comes from a psychologist or other nonmedical doctor, it can be helpful to share the report with the student's pediatrician, neurologist, or other treating doctor and ask that person to adopt the report in a cover letter, indicating that the student is being treated by a team of professionals who all concur with the recommendations. Once the documentation is obtained, it can be accompanied by a letter from the parent or guardian (an example is included in the following section).

Additionally, some students who have IEPs for ADHD during the school day may need 504 plans for afterschool and off-site programs offered by the school system. IEPs cover the school day, but some students need accommodations to enable them to participate in programs after school hours or off-campus.

It can be tempting for families who have researched ADHD to include every conceivable accommodation and related service they found in literature on the list of requests. However, each student is unique, and some interventions that are helpful for one child may be detrimental for another. Families should work closely with the professionals who have evaluated their child to develop recommendations designed to help their student succeed. They should also get input from the student, who can share what he or she would find helpful in the school setting.

## Sample Letter for Requesting a 504 Plan

Dear Guidance Counselor/504 Coordinator:

As the parent(s)/guardian(s) of (child's name), I/we would like to formally request that (child's name) be considered for a 504 plan to provide reasonable accommodations and related services for my/our child's disability/ies. Attached please find medical documentation from my/our child's treating doctor in support of my request. Please schedule a meeting with appropriate staff to discuss eligibility as soon as possible.

(Child's name) has many wonderful qualities, including
_____ . He (or she) also struggles with some skills, including _____ . I/we have noted the following that illustrates that (child's name) needs more support in the classroom.

(Child's name) needs accommodations and possibly related services in order to fully access the curriculum and services offered by your school. Our/my child's treating professionals have found the following to be necessary for school success: _____ . We also want to discuss with teachers and other school staff any recommendations they have that will help (child's name) flourish.

For afterschool programs and activities or field trips, my/our child needs _____ .

Please confirm receipt of this letter and let me/us know when the meeting can be arranged. The best times for me to meet are _____ . Please also let me/us know if you need any additional information in advance of the meeting.

I/We look forward to working with the school team on (child's name) behalf.

(Preferred friendly closing),
(Name/signature)
(Preferred contact information)

---

## CONSIDER THIS

Eight-year-old Eric was diagnosed with ADHD by his pediatrician. Eric was doing fairly well in school but was starting to fall below his peers in some areas. He was having trouble finishing his work at school, so his teacher routinely had him stay in for recess to complete any unfinished work. Eric's parents felt that taking that opportunity for movement away from Eric only made his afternoons worse. Furthermore, they felt he was overwhelmed with homework during the week. The parents took the diagnosis from the doctor to the 504 representative at the school and asked for a meeting to consider a 504. The team met and agreed Eric was struggling and needed a plan. Accommodations the team developed included not taking away all of Eric's recess, providing spelling words on Friday instead of Monday so he had longer to study, and reducing his homework.

## Navigating the Process to Consider Eligibility Under IDEA

Either you or the school asks for a meeting to consider eligibility for an IEP. Sometimes it may come up during a parent-teacher conference. If you are requesting the consideration, we recommend you put your request in writing to the Exceptional Student Education (ESE) coordinator. (See the sample letter included in this chapter.) If you do not hear back in a reasonable amount of time, say 10 school days, send a follow-up request. If you still do not get a response, contact the principal. In our experience it is always advantageous to work with the school staff, but if they are stonewalling your request, you will have to appeal to a district-level ESE coordinator. For the meeting and beyond:

1. Bring any documentation or records you may have. A formal evaluation is necessary for an eligibility. In our school district, an outside evaluation done by a private practitioner can be considered, but the school district always does some type of evaluation of its own. The school district has 60 school days from the time consent is signed to complete the testing. If it does not, it is considered to be out of compliance.
2. Keep track of the timeline and send a notice to the school if the 60-day period is approaching and you have not been invited to an eligibility/ineligibility meeting.
3. There are strict legal requirements about who participates in IEP meetings. Those present should include the parent, one

of your child's general education teachers, at least one special education teacher, a school psychologist or other person who can interpret the evaluation results, and a district representative. All of the pertinent information will be reviewed, and if it is determined that your child's ADHD affects his or her educational performance and he or she needs special education services, then an eligibility will be determined under Other Health Impairment, if there are no other comorbid diagnoses, such as a specific learning disability or an emotional disturbance.

4. The school staff and you write the IEP. IDEA requires that your child must be educated in the "least restrictive environment," meaning that he or she must be educated in a general education classroom setting as much as possible. Schools have different options for delivering educational services. Many have inclusion classrooms in which a special education teacher comes into the classroom for part of the day or the general education teacher is trained in techniques for instructing children with disabilities. Elsewhere, the child leaves the general education classroom for a portion of the day to receive instruction in areas in which he or she needs extra help. The IEP should include:

   - present levels of performance (i.e., how your child is doing in school);
   - annual educational goals established for any area in which your child is below grade level and procedures for how progress will be tracked;
   - services your child will receive (e.g., special education, supplementary speech or language assistance, an extended school year, etc.);
   - timing of the services (i.e., when they will start, how often they will happen, and how long they will be);
   - accommodations that may be necessary;
   - modifications as to what your child is expected to learn;

- whether or not your child will participate in state-mandated tests, which most children with ADHD do; and
- how much time your child will be in a general education classroom, which will likely be all or most of the day.

5. We recommend https://www.wrightslaw.com/info/iep.goals. plan.htm as a website where you can obtain information about effective IEP goals. The wording of the IEP is very important. Some districts create a draft IEP or shell before the meeting. If so, you should receive a copy in advance. If you feel you need additional time to review it, you don't have to sign the IEP at the meeting.

6. After the IEP is put into effect, try to monitor the effectiveness and whether or not the services are delivered as documented. The IEP is a legal document, so services should happen as described. The IEP is a living document, which can be changed as the child's needs change. It is reviewed annually, and a reevaluation of some type is required every 3 years.

Kimberly Spire-Oh provided the following information about IEPs and wrote a sample letter that you can utilize as you request services for your child with ADHD.

---

# Information and Sample Letter Requesting Consideration of an IEP

*By Kimberly Spire-Oh*

Although 504 plans are sufficient for quite a few students with ADHD, other students may need specialized instruction in order to perform well in all aspects of school. It is common for students with ADHD to struggle with executive functioning tasks, such as tackling large projects, keeping track of their assignments and school materials, and turning in homework on time. Schools can offer classes that provide students with coaching to help them develop coping mechanisms, help them keep track of their work completion and grades, and provide a class period in which assignments can be worked on and tests can be taken when extra time is needed. There are also social skills classes that can help students with ADHD learn strategies for effective interpersonal communication and dealing with their impulsivity. Due to difficulties focusing, students with ADHD may also benefit from inclusion classes with smaller teacher-to-student ratios, more repetition of concepts, and teaching by instructors experienced at presenting material in a variety of ways for students with different learning styles. All of these are examples of special education that requires an Individualized Education Plan (IEP).

Most students who need an IEP for ADHD obtain their eligibility through the Other Health Impaired (OHI) category. Each state sets the specific criteria for eligibility under each category, but many states require that a medical doctor provide documentation of a medical condition that significantly affects functioning in the educational environment. As with 504 plans, if the ADHD diagnosis and recommendations were provided by a psychologist or nonmedical doctor, the family can have the student's pediatrician or other treating doctor review and adopt the report in a cover letter that they sign. The family can then submit the medical documentation with a letter similar to the following, which will start the IEP evaluation process.

## Sample Letter for Requesting an IEP

Dear Special Education/Exceptional
Student Education Coordinator:

As the parent(s)/guardian(s) of (child's name), I/we would like to formally request that (child's name) be evaluated for special education eligibility and an Individualized Education Plan (IEP) for his/her Attention Deficit/Hyperactivity Disorder—Type_____ (and any other disabilities that impact education). Attached please find a letter/Other Health Impairment form from (child's name)'s treating physician. Please schedule an evaluation consent meeting within the next (10 school days or other timeframe, depending on your state's requirements) so that (child's name) receives his/her protections under the Child Find requirements of the Individuals with Disabilities Education Act (IDEA).

(Child's name) has many wonderful qualities, including _____ . S/he also struggles with some skills, including _____ . I/we have noted the following that illustrates that (child's name) needs special education services in order to achieve educational success.

I/we believe (Child's name) needs special education, accommodations, and possibly related services in order to fully access the curriculum and services offered by your school. Our/my child's treating professionals have found the following to be necessary for school success: _____ . We also want to discuss with teachers and other school staff any recommendations they have that will help (child's name) flourish.

For afterschool programs and activities or field trips, my/our child may also need a 504 plan to provide _____ .

Please confirm receipt of this letter and let me/us know when the meeting can be arranged. The best times for me to meet are _____ . Please also let me/us know if you need any additional information in advance of the meeting.

I/We look forward to working with the school team on (child's name) behalf.

(Preferred friendly closing),
(Name/signature)
(Preferred contact information)

## CONSIDER THIS

The Stallings were continually called to the school to confer about Alexa's misbehavior in her third-grade classroom. They were told she was constantly talking out of turn in the classroom, becoming upset if she did not receive help from the teacher immediately, and receiving failing grades on all of her written work. Mrs. Stallings was surprised because Alexa had not had problems to this extent in earlier grades. However, the Stallings understood impulsivity was a hallmark of Alexa's ADHD presentation. As soon as she had been diagnosed in second grade, they asked for a 504 plan to provide preferential seating near the teacher, frequent redirections back to tasks, and help with organizational skills.

Her 504 plan was updated to include a behavior plan to help Alexa and Mrs. Coates, her teacher, monitor the number of times she spoke out of turn. A small "stop" sign was laminated and put on her desk to remind her to stop and think before blurting out. She was also allowed to move to a quieter part of the room when completing her writing assignments, but Mrs. Coates would often find her gazing off into space rather than working on her papers. Alexa was also having significant difficulty keeping her belongings and materials organized. She often forgot to put papers where they belonged, lost homework, and forgot to have papers signed by her parents. Mrs. Coates felt overwhelmed by Alexa's needs. An IEP team was convened to review her work, her 504 plan, and its interventions. The team had parents sign permission for the school psychologist to do academic testing and behavior rating scales. The results showed Alexa's academic skills were on grade level, indicating her difficulty with her work was not attributable to a specific learning disability but to her ADHD. She was falling behind her peers, so an eligibility was declared for Other Health Impaired. Her diagnosis of ADHD had been on file since her diagnosis last year. An ESE teacher came into Mrs. Coates's room daily during the morning and again before dismissal to assist Alexa with her organizational skills.

# When Parents and the School Can't Reach an Agreement

## Advocates

Our experience has shown that most school districts try to meet the needs of their students. Occasionally, parents and the school reach an impasse. Often these situations can be hammered out at the school level.

*The most effective advocates we have seen understand different disabilities, can get a good overview of the situation, and advocate effectively for the best interests of the child.*

If needed, special education advocates who are knowledgeable about the law and the district processes can be very helpful. The most effective advocates we have seen understand different disabilities, can get a good overview of the situation, and advocate effectively for the best interests of the child. They can often be very effective in helping parents understand the complex process of eligibility and services available, as well as advocating for the child. Mary Anne has also seen cases in which the advocates helped parents be more realistic about what the school could provide. Their strong knowledge base about disabilities and educational law enables them to see the big picture and not get mired in the details. However, we have also been in meetings lasting 2 days because advocates were arguing minor points that were unimportant in the scheme of things.

## Lawyers

If you feel strongly that the district is not following the law, has not resolved issues with an advocate, and is not working for your child's best interest, hiring an attorney may be your next step. 504 and IDEA have specific provisions in the law for how disputes are to be resolved.

Education attorneys are usually brought in when the parent and the school district cannot resolve issues surrounding eligibility or services. If you plan to bring an attorney, you must notify the school prior to the meeting. The school will then have legal representation at the meeting. These meetings can last hours—even days—and can become quite contentious, but they are sometimes necessary to ensure the laws protecting your child are followed.

# What If I Don't Want to Label My Child?

Some parents are reluctant to create a "paper trail" and formalize their child's disability in the school's records, but it is better for your child's chronic problems to be understood for what they are—deficits in neurocognitive processes that affect day-to-day functioning. It's not laziness, lack of ability, or obstinacy. At times, early intervention provided through accommodations on a 504 plan could prevent the need for special education services later. The goal of a 504 plan or IDEA eligibility is not to provide a crutch or easy out for your child, but to enhance his or her chances of being successful by providing needed support.

# When Should My Child Be Aware of His or Her Disability?

Obviously, the answer to this question depends on many factors— the age of the child, ability to understand strengths and weaknesses, self-concept, and school environment. We feel it is important—and often comforting—for a child to understand areas in which he or she has strengths and challenges. Depending on your child's maturity, we recommend giving an age appropriate explanation and using the term ADHD for children ages 8 and older. Some children find it a relief to understand that there is a name for the symptoms they experience and that there are many ways they can receive help. We don't want them to use ADHD as a crutch and an excuse, but they should understand that if they address issues causing them problems, ADHD will not stand in the way of their success. Ultimately, our hope for all children with ADHD is that they are able to gain a clear picture of what helps them be successful and then advocate for themselves. Especially in middle and high school where teachers are dealing with so many students, it is helpful if students can let their teachers know what causes them difficulty and what helps them be successful.

*Some children find it a relief to understand that there is a name for the symptoms they experience and that there are many ways they can receive help.*

# What If My Child Doesn't Want to Be Treated Differently?

Some children are very resistant to use accommodations or additional help in the school setting because they don't want to be perceived as different from their peers. Especially in the upper grades of elementary school and middle school, fitting in is very important. It is important to be sensitive to that but also to help your child understand that each student's learning needs are unique. It is your job as parents to ensure that your child has opportunities he or she needs to be successful and view him- or herself as a capable learner. It is a balancing act to determine when to step in and insist that your child take advantage of assistance at school and when to try to support your child as he or she manages without the support. One thing is certain: If your child is not being successful, you and the school can work together to help him or her accept the help he or she needs. Our experience has shown that most teachers and schools are very sensitive to the stigma some children feel from being treated differently and try to minimize it as much as possible.

# Accommodations for the SAT/ACT

Requirements for receiving accommodations on the SAT and ACT with ADHD have become more stringent in recent years. In addition to a diagnosis, the student must provide a comprehensive evaluation that is not more than 3 years old and was completed by a licensed professional.

# The Importance of Establishing Eligibility Before College

Many students benefit from the structure provided at home and the efforts of elementary and secondary school faculties. When they get to college, they sometimes fall apart without those supports. If you suspect your child's ADHD might cause significant difficulty in college, it is important to establish eligibility for 504 or IDEA before she leaves secondary school, so her needs and accommodations will already be documented. The plans don't transfer to college, but they will document that your child previously qualified for supports.

Postsecondary institutions do provide accommodations and services but may require more information, such as updated testing. Once in college, your child will be expected to advocate for herself. Most colleges have disability coordinators who can provide guidance and support.

# Additional Resources

Valuable online resources include:

- "ADA Requirements: Testing Accommodations" by U.S. Department of Justice: https://www.ada.gov/regs2014/testing _accommodations.html
- OSERS: Office of Special Education and Rehabilitative Services: https://www2.ed.gov/about/offices/list/osers/osep/ index.html
- "The Difference Between IEPs and 504 plans" by The Understood Team: https://www.understood.org/en/school-learning/special-services/504-plan/the-difference-between-ieps-and-504-plans
- "What You Need to Know About IDEA 2004" by Wrightslaw: https://www.wrightslaw.com/idea/art.htm
- "Discrimination: Section 504 and ADA AA" by Wrightslaw: https://www.wrightslaw.com/info/sec504.index.htm
- "Ask the Advocate" by Pat Howey: https://www.wrightslaw. com/howey/ask.htm

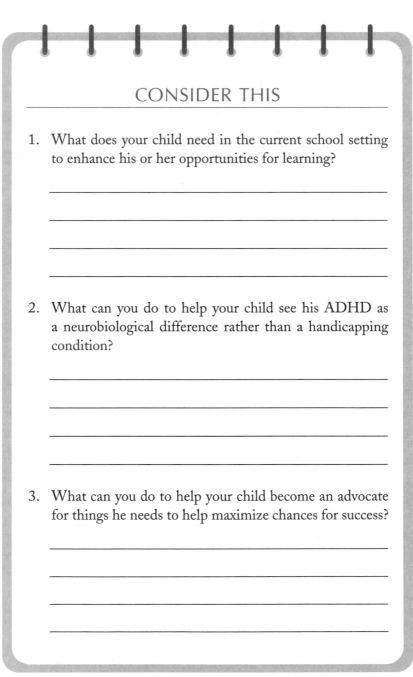

## CONSIDER THIS

1. What does your child need in the current school setting to enhance his or her opportunities for learning?

2. What can you do to help your child see his ADHD as a neurobiological difference rather than a handicapping condition?

3. What can you do to help your child become an advocate for things he needs to help maximize chances for success?

# Chapter 7

# Finding the Right Fit

The secret of change is to focus all of your energy, not on fighting the old, but on building the new. (Millman, 1984, p. 113)

Sometimes it seems our society is on choice overload. Even buying a box of cereal is confusing these days—so many choices with so many different ingredients. Schools are no different. There are more choices today than even before, which is a good thing. However, you have to be knowledgeable about your child's needs and which options might best fit those needs. As with anything, there is misinformation out there and biased opinions, so put on your detective hat to try to find the truth.

# Types of Schools

## Public Schools

Public schools are governed by school boards and adhere to state statutes and regulations. In Florida, for example, class sizes are governed by a class size amendment, so classes are a reasonable size. A large focus in public schools is preparation for and administration of mandated testing, but that could change as more parent groups are petitioning for less emphasis on testing. In many states, school grades are determined by student performance on mandated testing with particular emphasis on the lowest performing group of children. Most public schools have funding to be able to provide solid curriculum, and most teachers have some knowledge of disabilities and accommodations. Of course, IEPs or 504 plans are offered if your child qualifies.

## Magnet Schools

Magnet schools are public schools offering specialized courses at elementary, middle, and high school levels that are able to draw students outside their specified boundary areas. Magnet programs can include the arts, physical fitness and wellness, International Baccalaureate, business, and film, just to name a few.

## Charter Schools

Charter schools are public schools that receive government funding but are operated independently. They do not charge tuition and are mandated to provide free and appropriate public education (FAPE) for students with qualifying handicaps who have an IEP or 504 plan. They are governed by nonprofit boards and may differ in their procedures from public schools. For example, some charter schools have a policy of grade retention if grade-level standards are not met.

# Finding the Right Fight

## Virtual Schools

Virtual schools are publicly funded online schools offering personalized learning for public, private, and homeschooled students. Students may enroll full-time and receive all of their instruction or may register for specific courses to supplement their full-time school curriculum with permission from their school. For example, students may take a more advanced language course or a more interesting elective than offered at their school, an additional math class, or possibly a physical education class over the summer. They can also make up coursework, get ahead in credits or in some programs, qualify for industry certification. Students have interaction with a certified teacher and do most of their work on the computer. They can usually access the teacher via phone, e-mail, or text. Virtual schools can work well for students who are bored with a traditional classroom and want to go at a faster or slower pace. Consistent parental supervision, willingness to connect with the teacher at the appointed times, and a computer meeting the technical requirements of the program are required.

## Homeschooling

Homeschooling generally requires registering with the local school district for guidelines and requirements, which usually include an annual evaluation. For guidelines, you can contact your local school district or state department of education. It is important to have a comprehensive curriculum, supervision, and social opportunities with peers. Homeschooling can enable students to have a more individualized curriculum, little or no homework, hands-on learning, and opportunities for more movement. Many districts have homeschool cooperatives in which parents pool resources, arrange joint field trips, and share instruction. Jim knows firsthand that homeschooling can and does work for many children with ADHD. Some innovative private schools accommodate homeschool students for courses, such as providing science labs or specialized reading instruction, like Wilson Reading, offered on a weekly or daily basis.

### Specialized Day Schools

Specialized day schools cater to particular needs, such as behavior or learning, requiring a more specialized environment with a smaller teacher-to-student ratio. The teachers may have additional training in teaching and understanding students with ADHD, autism spectrum disorders, or behavioral disorders.

### Boarding Schools

Boarding schools cover a wide range of needs from sophisticated, college preparatory programs, to military schools, to therapeutic programs for children with serious emotional or behavioral problems who cannot be managed in their home setting. Because your child would be living away from home, it is important to thoroughly investigate the school and be very clear about the services offered, amount of supervision provided, and how misconduct is handled. Because finding the right fit for your child is so critical, we have found that many parents benefit from working with an educational consultant who specializes in boarding schools. Choose someone with in-depth knowledge about programs that have proven to be effective for students with ADHD. If your child attends a boarding school, it will be critical to stay in touch with the staff and your child to ensure all is going as planned and that your child is receiving the services you were promised.

# Tutoring

Tutors can make a world of difference for a struggling student. We have seen many students with ADHD who are so distractible in a large classroom setting that they miss large chunks of the instruction. Working one-on-one with a tutor, they are more able to focus, get questions answered, and demonstrate mastery of the subject. Tutors can vary in price depending on the area, so check online, with your local school, or other parents for information.

# Finding the Right Fight

Many schools allow their teachers to tutor as long as they are not tutoring a child under their care. The benefit of a tutor at the school your child attends is that he or she would be familiar with the curriculum and available to touch base with the child's teacher about problem areas to address during tutoring. We would encourage you to get recommendations from the school, teachers, and other parents. Because tutoring can be a long-term proposition, you want to find a good fit for your child—a tutor who is motivating, understands ADHD, and can explain the subject matter in an understandable way.

*Tutors can make a world of difference*
*for a struggling student.*

If your child has dyslexia, a very specific kind of tutoring in repetitive, systematic phonics is often recommended. The most well-known research-based programs include Orton-Gillingham, Wilson Reading, Lindamood-Bell, and Barton Reading and Spelling.

No-cost tutoring may be offered through your school, particularly if your child is considered to be below-grade-level and at-risk for not passing the mandated testing. In our local area, the National Junior Honor Society at several of our local high schools offers free tutoring one night a week for local elementary school students. Your local school may be able to advise you if there are any groups offering free tutoring in your area. Check with any colleges in your area, especially those offering degrees in education, to see if students might be required to tutor as part of their education. If there are no free services and you can't afford a certified tutor, some high school students can be very good tutors and work inexpensively. It would be important to make sure they understand your child's learning needs and how to help before you engage them.

Other tutoring options abound. Some parents like Kumon and Huntington Learning. Our experience has been that students often enjoy going because of the motivational systems that are part of their program. These programs usually do diagnostic testing to find out what your child's levels are so an instructional program can be designed around them. Make sure the program offered specifically meets your child's needs. Often your child will not have the same teacher from week to week, and tutoring may be done in a small group rather than on an individual basis.

# When Families Are Split

When families are split with shared custody and parents live in different school zones, they should choose the school that will serve their child most effectively by reviewing programs, school ratings, and input from parents who have children at the individual schools.

Children we have worked with benefit from parents having a united front about schedules, house rules, and homework. It is unfair for one parent to disregard homework and leave it up to the other to be the "enforcer" who sees to it that homework is completed. If you want your child to value education and be a lifelong learner, it is important for him to see that both parents value it.

*Children . . . benefit from parents having a united front about schedules, house rules, and homework.*

If possible, both homes should have a quiet study area. Consistent, reasonable bedtimes are important, so the child goes to school rested and ready to learn. The weekly schedule should be as consistent as possible. Children who alternate two school nights at one home and three at the other home and then reverse the pattern the following week can become easily confused about where they will be when. As difficult as it may be, try to give your child the best chance to succeed in school and select the most advantageous schedule for him or her.

# Additional Resources

Books for parents include:

- *Charter Schools: The Ultimate Handbook for Parents* by Karin Piper
- *How to Choose the Perfect School: What 21st Century Parents Need to Know About K–12 Education* by Mary Lang
- *Picky Parent Guide: Choose Your Child's School with Confidence, the Elementary Years (K–6)* by Bryan Hassel and Emily Ayscue Hassel
- *Schools That Learn: A Fifth Discipline Fieldbook for Educators, Parents, and Everyone Who Cares About Education* by Peter Senge, Nelda Cambron-McCabe, Timothy Lucas, Bryan Smith, Janis Dalton, and Art Kleiner
- *The Good School: How Smart Parents Get Their Kids the Education They Deserve* by Peg Tyre
- *What Effective Schools Do: Re-Envisioning the Correlates* by Lawrence Lezotte and Kathleen McKee Snyder

A valuable online resource is "Separating Fact From Fiction in 21 Claims About Charter Schools" by Valerie Strauss: https://www.washingtonpost.com/news/answer-sheet/wp/2015/02/28/separating-fact-from-fiction-in-21-claims-about-charter-schools.

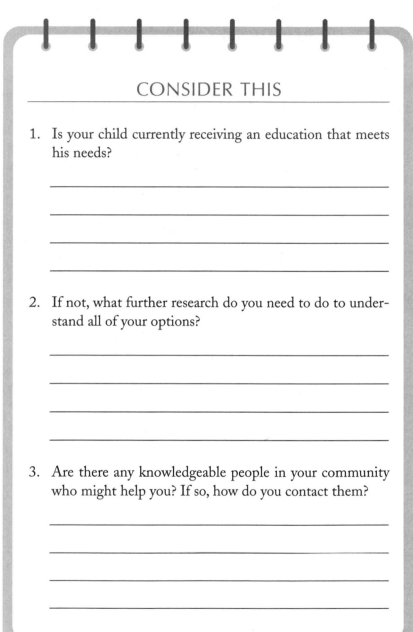

## CONSIDER THIS

1. Is your child currently receiving an education that meets his needs?

2. If not, what further research do you need to do to understand all of your options?

3. Are there any knowledgeable people in your community who might help you? If so, how do you contact them?

# Chapter 8

# The Success Plan

## Focused on the Future

Success is the doing, not the getting; in the trying, not the triumph. Success is a personal standard, reaching for the highest that is in us, becoming all that we can be. If we do our best, we are a success.

—Zig Ziglar

Now that you understand your child's Multiple Intelligences Profile and any Keys to Success that need strengthening, the next step is to take action. That is often easier said than done. However, as you know, your child's future is too important not to take action. We believe your child can reach his or her true potential.

Your child is a key part of the success plan, so you want him or her on board. Keep in mind that unlocking your child's potential unfolds over time, so although you may be eager to start a lot of new activities, maintain an even pace. You want to keep it enjoyable and avoid burnout. Choose activities that are manageable and beneficial; you and your child don't need more busywork.

*Unlocking your child's potential unfolds over time.*

Use the information you completed in Chapters 3 and 4 to give yourself a quick glance at how to proceed using the following Next Steps Chart.

## CONSIDER THIS

**Next Steps to Take**

| My Child's Top Intelligences | | |
|---|---|---|
| 1. | 2. | 3. |
| **Activities to Enhance:** | | |
| | | |
| | | |
| | | |

| Keys to Success That Need Strengthening | | |
|---|---|---|
| 1. | 2. | 3. |
| **Activities to Strengthen:** | | |
| | | |
| | | |
| | | |

# Working With Your Child to Ensure Success

If your child is 8 or older and you feel he is mature enough, we encourage you to give your child an age-appropriate explanation about his ADHD. Of course, it's a personal choice, and you may have already done this. In Jim's practices, he offers comprehensive ADHD testing for children and teens. When he meets with parents to discuss the results, he usually asks, "What will you tell your child?" They often do not know what to say, so he discusses age-appropriate explanations.

For the elementary-age child, we suggest explaining ADHD using dialogue like this:

> We met with the doctor and found out that you have so many strengths. You are smart, great at block building, and a strong thinker. We also found out why sometimes it is hard for you to pay attention and control your body. The doctor told us you have Attention Deficit/Hyperactivity Disorder, or ADHD. This means it is extra hard for you to keep your mind on things you are not really interested in doing and why your body can be so wiggly. There are a lot of things we will start doing to help you and us as a family. Do you have any questions?

For the middle or high school age child, we suggest using this dialogue:

> We met with the doctor and found out that you have so many strengths. You are smart, great at math, and a strong thinker. We also found out why sometimes it is hard for you to pay attention and control your impulses. The doctor told us you have Attention Deficit/Hyperactivity Disorder, or ADHD. You have probably heard of ADHD, right? It means there are certain brain chemicals that are not being produced in adequate supply. It's not anyone's fault that you have ADHD.

There are a lot of things we can consider to help you, like medication, coaching, or special supplements. You may even be able to have extra time on school tests. Do you have any questions?

During the conversation, we suggest telling the child that ADHD is not something he or she can use as an excuse to get out of doing work. Your child has to work just as hard as peers, if not harder, and can usually receive school accommodations. In our experience, most children have seen TV characters with ADHD or have friends with ADHD, so they usually have a general understanding of attention problems. The age-appropriate explanation helps your child understand that he or she is not broken or defective. Additionally, it helps your child understand how ADHD impacts her and what can be done to improve her life.

You may want to read your child a book to explain ADHD. Some examples include:

- *Learning to Slow Down and Pay Attention: A Book for Kids About ADHD* by Kathleen Nadeau and Ellen Dixon (ages 4–8)
- *What Were You Thinking?: Learning to Control Your Impulses* by Bryan Smith (ages 4–8)
- *The Survival Guide for Kids With ADHD* by John Taylor (ages 8–12)
- *Cory Stories: A Kid's Book About Living With ADHD* by Jeanne Kraus (ages 8–12)
- *The ADHD Workbook for Teens: Activities to Help You Gain Motivation and Confidence* by Lara Honos-Webb

# Maintaining Your Motivation

Our children with ADHD are consistently inconsistent in their behavior, academics, and performance. Thus, as a parent it is easy for you to feel discouraged when you have tried so hard, but things do not seem to be working out as you hoped. It's common to feel stuck in a rut—as parents, we've all been there. One way to maintain motivation during the down times is to reflect on how far you've come in raising your child.

> *One way to maintain motivation during the down times is to reflect on how far you've come in raising your child.*

Some families keep a memento box. Each time their child has a victory or reaches a milestone, they place an item in the box. This creates a permanent reminder of reaching a goal so that if you feel discouraged, you look in the box and see reminders of all of the progress. Other parents stay connected through ADHD support groups. Penny Williams is a mom, author, and ADHD and autism spectrum disorders advocate, who has a strong track record of supporting moms. She hosts mom events, including the Happy Mama Retreat and Purposeful Parent Boot Camp. She also maintains an active website (http://parentingadhdandautism.com) and offers individual coaching. Connecting with other moms or dads helps make parenting a child with ADHD less isolating. ImpactADHD (http://www.impactadhd.com) is another great resource for parents. It offers webinars, blogs, and interviews with experts in the field. Sanity School (https://sanityschool.com) is one of the popular programs offered for parents.

## CONSIDER THIS

Setting goals is crucial. In Chapter 1, you wrote down your dream for your child. Now it's time to set some goals for the future. Complete the following statements.

## CONSIDER THIS, *continued*

Today's date is _____ , and in 6 months, I want my child to _____ .

Today's date is _____ , and in 1 year, I want my child to _____ .

Now that you put your goals in writing, you have created a baseline for comparison. Perhaps you want to take a picture or write a Facebook post so that one year from now you may get a reminder. Or, use your smartphone to set a 6-month and a 12-month reminder to review your goals. You may be surprised how far you've progressed.

# Facing Difficulties

All children with ADHD have difficulties, and they occur on a continuum from mild to severe. You can manage many of your child's difficulties, such as disorganization, forgetfulness, or lack of personal hygiene, but some difficulties require outside support. These are challenges such as addictions to screen time, experimenting with drugs, or watching pornography. Some of our kids also have co-occurring conditions, such as anxiety or depression.

Melissa's son developed an addiction to screen time at age 13. She had to enroll him in an intensive outpatient addiction treatment program to help break the addiction. Her son would bypass the family's Internet network settings, steal his sister's tablet, and get devices from friends. Melissa and her husband would catch him in the middle of the night playing online games. When they took away his screens, he became violent and spewed curse words at them. This created extreme stress that affected his younger siblings. To complicate matters, Melissa and her husband, Dan, were not in agreement regarding disciplining their son. Dan believed it was okay to give him the screen time and refused to back up Melissa. Although it was not easy, through addiction counseling and parent meetings, they learned how to set limits and parent consistently. Even though it was much easier to give in to their son's behavior, they learned how to break the addiction cycle.

When your child experiences difficulty, remember to ask yourself, "Is this a 'won't' or a 'can't' issue?" If your child is having difficulty because he won't do something, then you know to invoke consequences. On the other hand, if your child can't do something, then you need to provide scaffolded teaching. David's high school age daughter had ADHD and was in a special education program at school. He wanted her to have practice in money management, so he gave her a credit card in her name from his account. She was able to drive and used the credit card to pay for gas at the pump. However, she was a repeat offender at losing her card. When she used the card, she then put it in a cup holder or tossed it in her purse. Somehow it disappeared. After the third cancelled card and many lengthy discussions, he determined that this wasn't a "can't" issue. She "won't" keep the card in the same safe location. Therefore, he took the card away, and when she needed gas, she had to ask him for cash.

# Monitoring Progress and Making Adjustments

If you've ever played a musical instrument, you understand adjustments or tuning are required. A musician can hear when her instrument is out of tune. Listen with your parenting ears, and you'll know when an adjustment is needed. Your child's education, social skills, study skills, mindset, attention, focus, and attitude all require monitoring and adjusting. After all, your child is growing and developing. We would neither want nor expect him to remain the same. We expect growth, and this causes growing pains.

You are going to frequently ask yourself, "Is my plan to unlock my child's potential working?" One way to assess progress is to refer back to the goals you set. Another way is to trust your parenting instinct. Remember, you are your child's shepherd. We set boundaries to help protect our children. We provide physical and emotional sustenance. We want them to be happy and on the right track toward independence. Just keep in mind that your plan for your child is not always your child's plan. Sometimes, you will have to make adjustments to your expectations.

*We expect growth, and this causes growing pains.*

Justin and Wanda's expectation for Paul, their son with ADHD, was always for him to attend college, but this was not Paul's plan. He told his parents that they would be wasting his time and their money. They thought a gap year might help him mature, and Paul agreed. The family looked online at gap year programs and even talked to a coordinator about a gap year in the Bahamas doing marine research. Paul agreed, so they put down a $500 deposit, and everyone was happy. Three months before the trip, Paul changed his mind and did not want to go away for a year because he would be "wasting" a year of his life. He wanted to go into full-time work. Justin and Wanda were stunned that their plan was not going to work out, but they recognized Paul was feeling anxious about leaving home and needed time to mature. They gave him 2 years to live at home and work full time.

# Final Thoughts

You should expect continuous improvement from your child as he or she grows into the person he or she is destined to become. Keep

## CONSIDER THIS

1. Where can you post your Next Steps chart?

   _____

   _____

   _____

   _____

   _____

2. Does your child understand ADHD?

   _____

   _____

   _____

   _____

   _____

3. Whom should you connect with for support?

   _____

   _____

   _____

   _____

   _____

the faith in your child—even when setbacks happen—because a child with ADHD is consistently inconsistent. Continue to speak the words and beliefs that encompass who you want your child to become. Your child is fortunate to have you as a parent, grandparent, guardian, or professional.

We'd like to close by thanking you for your effort and for the hard work you are doing for your child. Parents of kids with ADHD don't often hear many people say, "Thank you," but we know you deserve thanks. Helping your child make the most of his or her capabilities will be an accomplishment you can cherish all of your life. We can assure you that it is worth every ounce of effort you put into it. Our compassion goes out to you.

# References

Amen, D. (2013). *Healing ADD: The breakthrough program that allows you to see and heal the 7 types of ADD*. New York, NY: Berkley.

American Academy of Pediatrics. (2018). *Children and media tips from the Academy of Pediatrics*. Retrieved from https://www.aap.org/en-us/about-the-aap/aap-press-room/news-features-and-safety-tips/Pages/Children-and-Media-Tips.aspx

Americans with Disabilities Act, 42 U.S.C. §§ 12102 et seq. (1990).

Armstrong, T. (2009). *Multiple intelligences in the classroom* (3rd ed.). Alexandria, VA: ASCD.

Bailey, E. (2009). Interview with Howie Mandel. *Health Central*. Retrieved from https://www.healthcentral.com/article/interview-with-howie-mandel

Bailey, E. (2016). Wonder women: Meet six ADHD women who learned to own their ADHD symptoms and found success in the process. *ADDitude*. Retrieved from https://www.additudemag.com/adhd-wonder-women

Barkley, R. A. (1997). *ADHD and the nature of self-control*. New York, NY: Guilford Press.

Barkley, R. A. (2012). *Executive functions: What they are, how they work, and why they evolved.* New York, NY: Guilford Press.

Barkley, R. A., & Fischer, M. (2018). Hyperactive child syndrome and estimated life expectancy at young adult follow-up: The role of ADHD persistence and other potential predictors. *Journal of Attention Disorders.* https://doi.org/10.1177/1087054718816164

Biles, S. [Simone_Biles]. (2016, September 13). Having ADHD, and taking medicine for it is nothing to be ashamed of nothing that I'm afraid to let people know [Tweet]. Retrieved from https://twitter.com/Simone_Biles/status/775785767855611905

Bradshaw, T. (2001). *It's only a game.* New York, NY: Pocket Books.

Brenis, J. (2011). Jay Carter: ADHD hero. *ADHD Heroes.* Retrieved from https://www.adhdheros.org/2011/10/jay-carter-adhd-hero

Brooks, R., & Goldstein, S. (2001). *Raising resilient children: Fostering strength, hope, and optimism in your child.* Chicago, IL: Contemporary Books.

Brown, D. (2018). *Dawn Brown Psych MD.* Retrieved from http://drdawnpsychmd.com

Brown, T. E. (2013). *A new understanding of ADHD in children and adults: Executive function impairments.* New York, NY: Routledge.

Brown, T. E. (2014). *Smart but stuck: Emotions in teens and adults with ADHD.* San Francisco, CA: Jossey-Bass

Buningh, S. (2013, October). You're different, not defective: Actress Wendy Davis has a message about ADHD. *Attention,* 10–13.

Center for Public Education. (2011). *Time in school: How does the U.S. compare?* Retrieved from http://www.centerforpubliceducation.org/research/time-school-how-does-us-compare

Center on the Developing Child at Harvard University. (2011). *Building the brain's "air traffic control" system: How early experiences shape the development of executive function: Working paper No. 11.* Retrieved from http://developingchild.harvard.edu

Centers for Disease Control and Prevention. (2018). *Behavior therapy for young children with ADHD.* Retrieved from https://www.cdc.gov/ncbddd/adhd/behavior-therapy.html

# References

Chandler, S. (2001). *100 ways to motivate yourself: Change your life forever*. Franklin Lakes, NJ: Career Press.

CorePathway. (2013). *Dr Russell Barkley - ADHD motivation deficit disorder* [Video file]. Retrieved from https://www.youtube.com/watch?v=oTuqqExgX3s

Corman, C. A., & Hallowell, E. M. (2006). *Positively ADD: Real success stories to inspire your dreams*. New York, NY: Walker.

Cortese, S., Ferrin, M., Brandeis, D., Holtmann, M., Aggensteiner, P., Daley, D., . . . & Sonuga-Barke, E. J. (2016). Neurofeedback for Attention-Deficit/Hyperactivity Disorder: Meta-analysis of clinical and neuropsychological outcomes from randomized controlled trials. *Journal of the American Academy of Child & Adolescent Psychiatry, 55*, 444–455.

Dakessian, D. (2018, February). *Lowering the bar, but not too much: Figuring out how to work as a young woman with ADHD* [Web log post]. Retrieved from https://adhdrew.com/2018/02/19/how-to-work-as-a-young-woman-with-adhd

Davis, L. M. (2014). *A study of the factors associated with academic and vocational success in five women with co-occurring ADHD and LD* (Doctoral dissertation). Retrieved from ProQuest. (UMI No. 3665132)

Duckworth, A. (2016). *Grit: The power of passion and perseverance*. New York, NY: Scribner.

Duckworth, A. (2018). *Character lab*. Retrieved from https://www.characterlab.org

Durheim, M., & Zeigler Dendy, C. A. (2006). Educational laws regarding students with AD/HD. In C. A. Zeigler (Ed.), *CHADD educator's manual on attention-deficit/hyperactivity disorder (AD/HD): An in-depth look from an educational perspective* (pp. 125–134). Landover, MD: CHADD.

Dwyer Family Foundation. (2016). *For these celebrities, ADHD was not an impediment*. Retrieved from http://dwyerfamilyfoundation.com/for-these-celebrities-adhd-was-not-an-impediment

Edge Foundation. (2017). *Ty Pennington's extreme ADHD make-over*. Retrieved from https://edgefoundation.org/2017/04/15/ ty-penningtons-extreme-adhd-makeover

Forgan, J. W., & Richey, M. A. (2012). *Raising boys with ADHD: Secrets for parenting happy, healthy sons*. Waco, TX: Prufrock Press.

Forgan, J. W., & Richey, M. A. (2015). *The impulsive, disorganized child: Solutions for parenting kids with executive functioning difficulties*. Waco, TX: Prufrock Press.

Gardner, H. (1983). *Frames of mind: The theory of multiple intelligences*. New York, NY: Basic Books.

Gardner, H. (1995). Reflections on multiple intelligences myths and messages. *Phi Delta Kappan, 77*, 200–203, 206–209.

Gerber, P. J., & Ginsberg, R. J. (1990). *Identifying alterable patterns of success in highly successful adults with learning disabilities. Executive summary*. Richmond: Virginia Commonwealth University School of Education.

Gilman, L. (2004/2005). How to succeed in business with ADHD. *ADDitude*. Retrieved from https://www.additudemag.com/adhd-entrepreneur-stories-jetblue-kinkos-jupitermedia

Ginsburg, K., & Jablow, M. (2011). *Building resilience in children and teens: Giving kids roots and wings* (2nd ed.). Elk Grove Village, IL: American Academy of Pediatricians.

Goalcast. (2017). *David Blaine: The secret of magic is practice* [Video file]. Retrieved from https://www.goalcast.com/2017/03/14/david-blaine-secret-magic-practice

Goldberg, R. J., Higgins, E. L., Raskind, M. H., & Herman, K. L. (2003). Predictors of success in individuals with learning disabilities: A qualitative analysis of a 20-year longitudinal study. *Learning Disabilities Research & Practice, 18*, 222–236.

Haskell, R. (2014). Channing Tatum: A work in progress. *The New York Times Style Magazine*. Retrieved from https://www.nytimes. com/2014/10/14/t-magazine/channing-tatum-foxcatcher-interview.html

# References

Hiroto, D. S., & Seligman, M. E. (1975). Generality of learned help-lessness in man. *Journal of Personality and Social Psychology, 31*, 311–327.

Hodgson, K., Hutchinson, A. D., & Denson, L. (2012). Non-pharmacological treatments for ADHD: A meta-analytic review. *Journal of Attention Disorders, 17*, 275–282.

Individuals with Disabilities Education Act, 20 U.S.C. §1401 et seq. (1990).

Individuals with Disabilities Education Improvement Act, Pub. Law 108-446 (December 3, 2004).

International Society for Neurofeedback and Research. (2010). *Definition of neurofeedback.* Retrieved from https://www.isnr.org/neurofeedback-introduction

Jamieson, K. (2018). Resilience: A powerful weapon in the fight against ACEs. *Center for Child Counseling.* Retrieved from https://www.centerforchildcounseling.org/resilience-a-powerful-weapon-in-the-fight-against-aces

Jang, M. (2015). iHeartRadio Awards 2015: Justin Timberlake addresses critics, says "their words will fade." *The Hollywood Reporter.* Retrieved from https://www.hollywoodreporter.com/news/justin-timberlake-receives-innovator-award-785158

Javier, J. (2018). Nurturing parent-child relationships. *The University of Arizona Alumni Association.* Retrieved from http://arizonaalumni.com/article/nurturing-parent-child-relationships

JimCaviezel.us. (1998–2017). *Trivia.* Retrieved from http://www.jimcaviezel.us/trivia.html

Kabat-Zinn, J. (2003). Mindfulness-based interventions in context: Past, present, and future. *Clinical Psychology: Science and Practice, 10*, 144–156.

Kaleidoscope Society. (2016). *How an ADHD diagnosis at 41 helped Toya take the leap.* Retrieved from http://www.kaleidoscopesociety.com/toya

Kirby, D. (2008). Higher education, ADHD and the creation of student entrepreneurs: Is there a need to rethink? *Journal of Asia Entrepreneurship and Sustainability, 4*, 110–122.

Krishnan, K., & Meltzer, L. (2014). *Executive function: Organizing and prioritizing strategies for academic success.* Retrieved from http://www.ncld.org/types-learning-disabilities/executive-function-disorders/ executive-functioning-organizing-prioritizing

Kubik, J. A. (2010). Efficacy of ADHD coaching for adults with ADHD. *Journal of Attention Disorders, 13,* 442–453.

Kutscher, M. L., & Rosin, N. (2015, June). Too much screen time? When your child with ADHD over-connects to technology. *Attention, 22–25.*

Lavoie, R. (2007). *The motivation breakthrough: 6 secrets to turning on the tuned-out child.* New York, NY: Simon & Schuster.

Levine, M. (2002). *A mind at a time.* New York, NY: Simon & Schuster.

Lofthouse, N., Arnold, L. E., Hersch, S., Hurt, E., & DeBeus, R. (2012). A review of neurofeedback treatment for pediatric ADHD. *Journal of Attention Disorders, 16,* 351–372.

Maitland, T. E., & Quinn, P. O. (2011). *Ready for take-off: Preparing your teen with ADHD or LD for college.* Washington, DC: Magination Press.

Mandel, H. (2010). "I have a tough time being with myself." *ADDitude.* Retrieved from https://www.additudemag.com/howie-mandel-ocd

Marrero, L. (2018). How to promote resourcefulness in yourself and others. *Lifehack.* Retrieved from https://www.lifehack.org/ articles/featured/how-to-promote-resourcefulness-in-yourself-and-others.html

Mayes, S. D., & Calhoun, S. L. (2007). Wechsler Intelligence Scale for Children-Third and -Fourth Edition predictors of academic achievement in children with attention-deficit/hyperactivity disorder. *School Psychology Quarterly, 22,* 234–249. http://dx.doi.org/10.1037/1045-3830.22.2.234

Mbe, V. S. (2017). David Blaine: The magic of making the impossible, real. *ThoughtEconomics.* Retrieved from https://thoughteconomics.com/david-blaine-interview

Mejia, Z. (2018). Actor Will Smith in viral video: 'Failure is a massive part of being able to be successful'. *CNBC.* Retrieved from https://

# References

www.cnbc.com/2018/01/24/will-smith-failure-is-a-massive-part-of-being-able-to-be-successful.html

Meltzer, L. (2010). *Promoting executive function in the classroom.* New York, NY: Guilford Press.

Merriman, D. E., & Codding, R. S. (2008). The effects of coaching on mathematics homework completion and accuracy of high school students with attention-deficit/hyperactivity disorder. *Journal of Behavioral Education, 17,* 339.

Millman, D. (1984). *Way of the peaceful warrior. A book that changes lives.* Tiburon, CA: Kramer.

Moran, S., Kornhaber, M., & Gardner, H. (2009). Orchestrating multiple intelligences. In K. Ryan & M. Cooper, *Kaleidoscope: Contemporary and classic readings in education* (12th ed., pp. 188–192). Belmont, CA: Wadsworth.

MulliganBrothers. (2014). *Jim Carrey – Motivational speech* [Video file]. Retrieved from https://www.youtube.com/watchv=?_okUPXY7H hU

Multimodal Treatment Study of Children with ADHD Cooperative Group. (1999). A 14-month randomized clinical trial of treatment strategies for attention-deficit/hyperactivity disorder. *Archives of General Psychiatry, 56,* 1073–1086.

Nadeau, K. (2017). *Still distracted after all these years: Exploring ADHD after 60* [Web log post]. https://apsard.org/still-distracted-after-all-these-years-exploring-adhd-after-60

Parenting.com. (2014). *Superstar interview: Michael Phelps.* Retrieved from https://www.parenting.com/article/superstar-interview-michael-phelps

Petersen, N. (2016, May). *3 ways you can make a difference for a kid with ADHD* [Web log post]. Retrieved from https://blogs.psych central.com/adhd-millennial/2016/05/3-ways-you-can-make-a-difference-for-a-kid-with-adhd

Poirier-Leroy, O. P. (2016). 5 things Michael Phelps taught me about swimming and success in life. *YourSwimBook.* Retrieved from https://www.yourswimlog.com/5-things-michael-phelps-taught-swimming-success-life

Prevatt, F., & Young, J. L. (2014). Recognizing and treating attention-deficit/hyperactivity disorder in college students. *Journal of College Student Psychotherapy, 28,* 182–200.

Proulx-Schirduan, V., Shearer, C. B., & Case, K. I. (2009). Mindful education for ADHD students: Differentiating curriculum and instruction using multiple intelligences. New York, NY: Teachers College Press.

Purdie, N., Hattie, J., & Carroll, A. (2002). A review of the research on interventions for attention deficit hyperactivity disorder: What works best? *Review of Educational Research, 72,* 61–99.

Raskind, M. H., Goldberg, R. J., Higgins, E. L., & Herman, K. L. (1999). Patterns of change and predictors of success in individuals with learning disabilities: Results from a twenty-year longitudinal study. *Learning Disabilities Research & Practice, 14*(1), 35–49.

Redfearn, S. (2017). A giant accomplishment. *ADDitude.* Retrieved from https://www.additudemag.com/a-giant-accomplishment

Reynolds, J. L. (2017). Good habits of successful people with ADHD. *U.S. News.* Retrieved from https://health.usnews.com/health-care/patient-advice/articles/2017-06-23/good-habits-of-successful-people-with-adhd

Salimpoor, V. N., Benovoy, M., Larcher, K., Dagher, A., & Zatorre, R. J. (2011). Anatomically distinct dopamine release during anticipation and experience of peak emotion to music. *Nature Neuroscience, 14,* 257.

Savage, S. (2008). *Celebrity designer and ADHD spokesperson Ty Pennington partners with Shire to Announce the launch of VYVANSE(TM) (lisdexamfetamine dimesylate) for the treatment of ADHD in adults.* Retrieved from https://www.redorbit.com/news/health/1489259/celebrity_designer_and_adhd_spokesperson_ty_pennington_partners_with_shire

Section 504 of the Rehabilitation Act, 29 U.S.C. Section 706 et. Seq. (1973).

Shoot, B. (2011). The stars who aligned ADHD with success. *ADDitude.* Retrieved from https://www.additudemag.com/successful-people-with-adhd-learning-disabilities

# References

Sibley, M. H., & Yeguez, C. E. (2018, May). Managing ADHD at the post-secondary transition: A qualitative study of parent and young adult perspectives. *School Mental Health*, 1–20.

Siegel, D. J., & Bryson, T. P. (2018). *The yes brain child: Help your child be more resilient, independent and creative.* London, England: Simon & Schuster.

Silverman, R. (2017, May). How a CEO with dyslexia and ADHD runs his company. *Wall Street Journal.* Retrieved from https://www.wsj.com/articles/how-a-ceo-with-dyslexia-and-adhd-runs-his-company-1494952535

Sonuga-Barke, E. J., Brandeis, D., Cortese, S., Daley, D., Ferrin, M., Holtmann, M., ... & Dittmann, R. W. (2013). Nonpharmacological interventions for ADHD: Systematic review and meta-analyses of randomized controlled trials of dietary and psychological treatments. *American Journal of Psychiatry, 170,* 275–289.

Spekman, N. J., Goldberg, R. J., & Herman, K. L. (1992). Learning disabled children grow up: A search for factors related to success in the young adult years. *Learning Disabilities Research & Practice, 7,* 161–170.

Spekman, N. J., Goldberg, R. J., & Herman, K. L. (1993). An exploration of risk and resilience in the lives of individuals with learning disabilities. *Learning Disabilities Research & Practice, 8,* 11–18.

Starr, L. B. (n.d.). *Simone Biles' secret to Olympic success.* Retrieved from http://www.futureofpersonalhealth.com/advocacy/simone-biles-secret-to-olympic-success

Stockett, K. (2009). *The help.* New York, NY: Berkley Books.

Subcommittee on Attention-Deficit/Hyperactivity Disorder, Steering Committee on Quality Improvement and Management. (2011). ADHD: Clinical practice guideline for the diagnosis, evaluation and treatment attention-deficit/hyperactivity disorder in children and adolescents. *Pediatrics, 128,* 1–18.

Sulkowski, M., & Picciolini, C. (2018). The path into and out of violent extremism—Part 1: How youth become radicalized into violent extremism. *Communique, 47,* 17–19.

Sulla, E. (2017). *Examining intra-personal and external support factors supporting academic success in post-secondary students with ADHD* (Doctoral dissertation). Retrieved from https://era.library.ualberta.ca/items/3f5425f9-cc69-4c0f-90ec-ca2684574cb3

Teeter, P. A. (1998). *Interventions for ADHD: Treatment in developmental context.* New York, NY: Guilford Press.

TyPennington.com. (n.d.). *About Ty.* Retrieved from https://typennington.com/about-ty-pennington

van der Oord, S., Bogels, S. M., & Peijnenburg, D. (2012). The effectiveness of mindfulness training for children with ADHD and mindful parenting for their parents. *Journal of Child and Family Studies, 21,* 139–147.

Wallace, J. B. (2015). Why children need chores. *The Wall Street Journal.* Retrieved from https://www.wsj.com/articles/why-children-need-chores-1426262655

Werner, E. E. (1993). Risk and resilience in individuals with learning disabilities: Lessons learned from the Kauai longitudinal study. *Learning Disabilities Research & Practice, 8,* 28–34.

Wickelgren, I. (2011, September). *Goldie Hawn plunges into brain science* [Web log post]. Retrieved from https://blogs.scientificamerican.com/streams-of-consciousness/goldie-hawn-plunges-into-brain-science

# Success Surveys

The Multiple Intelligences Profile and Keys to Success Survey are included in this appendix. Downloadable PDF versions of the two tools are also available at https://www.prufrock.com/The-ADHD-Empowerment-Guide-Resources.aspx.

# Multiple Intelligences Profile

Name: _____ Age: _____ Grade: _____

**Directions:** Think about your child's natural affinities and talents. Circle the number that best represents your child in each of the categories that follow.

1 = not at all like my child
2 = low characteristic of my child
3 = medium characteristic of my child
4 = high characteristic of my child

| Visual-Spatial Intelligence | N/A | Low | Med | High |
|---|---|---|---|---|
| Quickly identifies how parts fit together to make a whole; enjoys puzzles and/or building (e.g., LEGOs, Magna-Tiles, K'Nex) or playing computer games (e.g., Minecraft or Roblox) | 1 | 2 | 3 | 4 |
| Remembers places and directions to get to places | 1 | 2 | 3 | 4 |
| Has a good understanding of design and spatial relationships, such as the layout of a room or what colors and designs go together | 1 | 2 | 3 | 4 |
| Has a good sense of directionality (e.g., can differentiate right from left or understands north, south, east, and west) | 1 | 2 | 3 | 4 |
| Understands and remembers pictures better than words (e.g., may prefer to draw a picture about a story rather than write it or can follow visual directions with pictures easier than words) | 1 | 2 | 3 | 4 |
| Total Score: | | | | |

| Bodily-Kinesthetic Intelligence | N/A | Low | Med | High |
|---|---|---|---|---|
| Enjoys participating in sports, either team or individual | 1 | 2 | 3 | 4 |
| Prefers and/or learns best through hands-on activities | 1 | 2 | 3 | 4 |

# Appendix A

*Multiple Intelligences Profile, continued*

| Bodily-Kinesthetic Intelligence, *continued* | N/A | Low | Med | High |
|---|---|---|---|---|
| Can learn a series of body movements easily, such as a dance, gymnastics, or karate routine, or swinging a golf club or bat | 1 | 2 | 3 | 4 |
| Is agile or well-coordinated (e.g., can jump rope, ride a bicycle, or skateboard) | 1 | 2 | 3 | 4 |
| Learns through movement; may prefer to stand by his or her desk or walk around while studying | 1 | 2 | 3 | 4 |
| Total Score: | | | | |

| Linguistic Intelligence | N/A | Low | Med | High |
|---|---|---|---|---|
| Talked at an early age (e. g., spoke first words before 1 year of age and was noticeably advanced in speaking in sentences) and enjoys talking | 1 | 2 | 3 | 4 |
| Likes being read to or reading books | 1 | 2 | 3 | 4 |
| Enjoys words games or easily picks up foreign languages when exposed | 1 | 2 | 3 | 4 |
| Easily remembers quotes, sayings, or lines from movies | 1 | 2 | 3 | 4 |
| Has an advanced vocabulary | 1 | 2 | 3 | 4 |
| Total Score: | | | | |

| Interpersonal Intelligence | N/A | Low | Med | High |
|---|---|---|---|---|
| Eagerly engages with other people, children or adults (e.g., starts conversations with unfamiliar children, is comfortable talking to adults) | 1 | 2 | 3 | 4 |
| Is sensitive to others' emotions; is intuitive about people and knows how to identify who might make a good friend; handles situations that arise in friendships | 1 | 2 | 3 | 4 |
| Is cooperative in groups (e.g., enjoys clubs, committees, or team activities) | 1 | 2 | 3 | 4 |
| Has two or more close friends | 1 | 2 | 3 | 4 |
| Demonstrates a good sense of humor (e.g., funny, witty, can get others to laugh) | 1 | 2 | 3 | 4 |
| Total Score: | | | | |

*Multiple Intelligences Profile, continued*

| Logical Intelligence | N/A | Low | Med | High |
|---|---|---|---|---|
| Interested in how things work (e.g., conducting science experiments or chasing down solutions when things don't work) | 1 | 2 | 3 | 4 |
| Has a good sense of cause and effect (e.g., if you jump from the top of a swing set, you are likely to get hurt; if you yell at someone, he or she may be upset) | 1 | 2 | 3 | 4 |
| Is able to see the big picture and seeks rational explanations | 1 | 2 | 3 | 4 |
| Is good at strategy games, logic puzzles, and brain teasers | 1 | 2 | 3 | 4 |
| Is good at math, operating a computer, and learning coding | 1 | 2 | 3 | 4 |
| Total Score: | | | | |

| Musical Intelligence | N/A | Low | Med | High |
|---|---|---|---|---|
| Easily memorizes songs or lyrics and may show a good sense of rhythm | 1 | 2 | 3 | 4 |
| Is talented with an instrument or voice | 1 | 2 | 3 | 4 |
| Enjoys listening and is sensitive to music (e.g., can be energized or calmed by music) | 1 | 2 | 3 | 4 |
| Enjoys participating in musical activities, whether individual or group (e.g., choir, glee club, or band) | 1 | 2 | 3 | 4 |
| Likes to watch music videos, music-related TV shows, and performances | 1 | 2 | 3 | 4 |
| Total Score: | | | | |

# Appendix A

| Intrapersonal Intelligence | N/A | Low | Med | High |
|---|---|---|---|---|
| Has an understanding and acceptance of own strengths and weaknesses (e.g., acknowledges he or she may be better at math than reading or may be better at art than athletics) | 1 | 2 | 3 | 4 |
| Understands his or her status within different activities (e.g., knows when to be a leader or a support person in different situations) | 1 | 2 | 3 | 4 |
| Has a sense of self-identity and a personal style (e.g., not influenced by others' opinions) | 1 | 2 | 3 | 4 |
| Is comfortable playing or working alone (e.g., spends time thinking or may enjoy journaling) | 1 | 2 | 3 | 4 |
| Is independent and prefers to do things without assistance | 1 | 2 | 3 | 4 |
| Total Score: | | | | |

| Naturalistic Intelligence | N/A | Low | Med | High |
|---|---|---|---|---|
| Prefers to be outside and feels comfortable in nature as opposed to being indoors | 1 | 2 | 3 | 4 |
| Is interested in animals and plants (e.g., likes Discovery Channel, YouTube nature videos, or books about animals and plants) | 1 | 2 | 3 | 4 |
| Is conscious of and reacts to weather changes | 1 | 2 | 3 | 4 |
| Is aware of nature and is sensitive to surroundings | 1 | 2 | 3 | 4 |
| Has well-developed sensory skills for experiencing nature (e.g., can identify animals by their calls, enjoys playing in dirt and sand, and uses senses to explore nature) | 1 | 2 | 3 | 4 |
| Total Score: | | | | |

# Multiple Intelligences
# Profile Scoring Sheet

**Directions:** Record your child's total for each intelligence category on the chart below. Graph the results. Then, identify your child's top three scores.

Name: _____

Top Intelligences:
1. _____
2. _____
3. _____

| 20 | | | | | | | | |
|---|---|---|---|---|---|---|---|---|
| 15 | | | | | | | | |
| 10 | | | | | | | | |
| 5 | | | | | | | | |
| | Visual-Spatial | Bodily-Kinesthetic | Linguistic | Interpersonal | Logical | Musical | Intrapersonal | Naturalistic |

# Keys to Success Survey

Name: _____ Age: _____ Grade: _____

**Directions:** Think about your child and circle the number that best represents your child in each of the following categories.

1 = not at all like my child
2 = low characteristic of my child
3 = medium characteristic of my child
4 = high characteristic of my child

## Internal Keys to Success

| Motivation | N/A | Low | Med | High |
|---|---|---|---|---|
| Has the drive to achieve and understands effort can produce results (e.g., a struggling reader understands tutoring helps so he works hard) | 1 | 2 | 3 | 4 |
| Is a self-starter and takes action | 1 | 2 | 3 | 4 |
| Gains momentum and a sense of pride through success | 1 | 2 | 3 | 4 |
| Finds pleasure in working in a chosen area and pursues activities related to it (e.g., a child who is a good reader and constantly wants to read, a child with ADHD who enjoys woodshop and studies general contracting) | 1 | 2 | 3 | 4 |
| Total Score: | | | | |

| Emotional Stability and Behavioral Control | N/A | Low | Med | High |
|---|---|---|---|---|
| Usually maintains an even disposition | 1 | 2 | 3 | 4 |
| Is developing self-control | 1 | 2 | 3 | 4 |
| Has coping strategies (e.g., ways to calm down, self-talk, breathing, or removing him- or herself from the situation) | 1 | 2 | 3 | 4 |

*Keys to Success Survey, continued*

| Emotional Stability and Behavioral Control, *continued* | N/A | Low | Med | High |
|---|---|---|---|---|
| Thinks before acting (e.g., looks before crossing street, waits his or her turn, listens for direction before starting task) | 1 | 2 | 3 | 4 |
| Total Score: | | | | |

| Integrity | N/A | Low | Med | High |
|---|---|---|---|---|
| Is honest (e.g., does not cheat, steal, or lie) | 1 | 2 | 3 | 4 |
| Respects others (e.g., is tolerant of others' ideas; doesn't hit, name call, or bully; accepts winning and losing) | 1 | 2 | 3 | 4 |
| Takes responsibility for actions—both positive and negative outcomes (e.g., accepts recognition for a good job, admits wrongdoing, apologizes when needed) | 1 | 2 | 3 | 4 |
| Follows through on promises and commitments | 1 | 2 | 3 | 4 |
| Total Score: | | | | |

| Social Skills | N/A | Low | Med | High |
|---|---|---|---|---|
| Communicates effectively through oral communication (talking) and body language | 1 | 2 | 3 | 4 |
| Cooperates with others and contributes to group efforts | 1 | 2 | 3 | 4 |
| Can identify and express feelings, such as frustration, in a socially appropriate manner | 1 | 2 | 3 | 4 |
| For younger children: Understands and respects boundaries of personal space<br>For children 10 or older: Is able to observe and pick up social cues in the environment by observing others and responding appropriately to them | 1 | 2 | 3 | 4 |
| Total Score: | | | | |

# Appendix A

*Keys to Success Survey, continued*

| Grit | N/A | Low | Med | High |
|---|---|---|---|---|
| Shows perseverance and handles obstacles without making excuses or giving up (e.g., a child with ADHD often doesn't like the effort required in writing and may not be good at it but does it anyway without significant complaining) | 1 | 2 | 3 | 4 |
| Is motivated and feels a sense of accomplishment in completing tasks (e.g., child starts and finishes tasks independently) | 1 | 2 | 3 | 4 |
| Can set small goals with assistance and work toward them with an incentive (e.g., a child with ADHD starts homework without parent nagging, a child works to improve classroom behavior to receive adult praise or reward, an older child is motivated by money and creates an idea for earning it) | 1 | 2 | 3 | 4 |
| Is passionate and committed to one or more interests for an age-appropriate time period (e.g., starts playing an instrument or on a sports team and does not quit) | 1 | 2 | 3 | 4 |
| Total Score: | | | | |

| Organization | N/A | Low | Med | High |
|---|---|---|---|---|
| Manages materials required for a task | 1 | 2 | 3 | 4 |
| Is able to make and follow a schedule | 1 | 2 | 3 | 4 |
| Can keep up with and meet deadlines | 1 | 2 | 3 | 4 |
| Keeps an orderly room and work space | 1 | 2 | 3 | 4 |
| Total Score: | | | | |

| Resilience | N/A | Low | Med | High |
|---|---|---|---|---|
| Bounces back from failure | 1 | 2 | 3 | 4 |
| Learns and grows from mistakes (e.g., has a growth mindset and understands that experiences can foster learning and growth) | 1 | 2 | 3 | 4 |
| Can reappraise situations and regulate emotions | 1 | 2 | 3 | 4 |
| Is generally optimistic | 1 | 2 | 3 | 4 |
| Total Score: | | | | |

*Keys to Success Survey, continued*

| Resourcefulness | N/A | Low | Med | High |
|---|---|---|---|---|
| Is a problem solver (e.g., is flexible in his or her thinking and comes up with alternatives when things don't work as planned) | 1 | 2 | 3 | 4 |
| Understands the overall scope and requirements of an activity and can take on different roles as required (e.g., can be a leader or a good team member) | 1 | 2 | 3 | 4 |
| Thinks creatively and outside the box | 1 | 2 | 3 | 4 |
| Adapts to new or difficult situations | 1 | 2 | 3 | 4 |
| Total Score: | | | | |

## External Keys to Success

| Appropriate School Setting | N/A | Low | Med | High |
|---|---|---|---|---|
| Has a school environment that supports his or her academic needs (e.g., 504 or IEP is in place if needed and followed, teacher understands and values my child) | 1 | 2 | 3 | 4 |
| Is capable of doing the academic work | 1 | 2 | 3 | 4 |
| Has friends and is socially accepted and comfortable | 1 | 2 | 3 | 4 |
| Has a school environment that contributes to his or her success | 1 | 2 | 3 | 4 |
| Total Score: | | | | |

| Support Systems | N/A | Low | Med | High |
|---|---|---|---|---|
| Has one or more people who believe in and help bring out the best in him or her | 1 | 2 | 3 | 4 |
| Has one or more people who spend quality time with him or her | 1 | 2 | 3 | 4 |
| Asks for support when needed | 1 | 2 | 3 | 4 |
| Has people in the school setting who don't give up on him or her | 1 | 2 | 3 | 4 |
| Total Score: | | | | |

# Appendix A

*Keys to Success Survey, continued*

| Productive Use of Technology* | N/A | Low | Med | High |
|---|---|---|---|---|
| Uses technology to independently get up in the morning | 1 | 2 | 3 | 4 |
| Uses technology to set reminders of due dates for assignments, important tests or projects, or scheduled activities | 1 | 2 | 3 | 4 |
| Uses technology to monitor school assignments and keep track of grades | 1 | 2 | 3 | 4 |
| Uses technology for learning, (e.g., Quizlet for making flash cards or taking a practice test, or watching YouTube videos or Kahn Academy to learn new skills) | 1 | 2 | 3 | 4 |
| Total Score: | | | | |

*This key is primarily for ages 13-16.

# Keys to Success Survey Scoring Sheet

**Directions:** Record your child's total for each characteristic on the chart below. Graph the results. Then, identify your child's weakest areas.

Child's Name: _____

Choose your child's three
weakest areas to strengthen:

1. _____
2. _____
3. _____

**Keys
to
Success**

16
12
8
4

Motivaton

Emotional Stability
and Behavioral Control

Integrity

Social Skills

Grit

Organization

Resilience

Resourcefulness

Appropriate School Setting

Support Systems

Use of Technology

# Coping Menu

# COPING MENU

**My worries come and go, and they are okay to have.
I can think of safe things to do if I have worries.**

Take Deep Breaths

Count to 10

Talk to Someone About It

Give a Hug

*Coping Menu, continued*

*Coping Menu, continued*

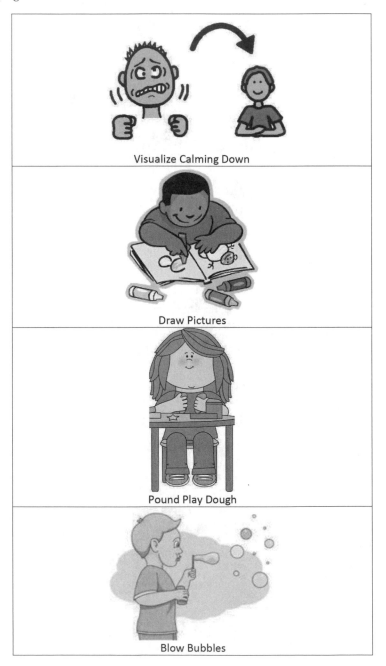

Visualize Calming Down

Draw Pictures

Pound Play Dough

Blow Bubbles

*Coping Menu, continued*

Listen to Relaxing Music

Go to a Quiet Space

Sing a Song

Use a Stress Thermometer

*Coping Menu, continued*

Look at Pictures of Family, Friends, or Pets

Hold Small Toy or Stuffed Animal

Write About It

Squeeze a Stress Ball

# Appendix B

*Coping Menu, continued*

Listen to a Mindfulness Recording

Meditate

© 2017 Rachel Salinger

*Note.* Reprinted with permission of the author.

# About the Authors

James W. Forgan and Mary Anne Richey have spent a combined 67 years working with children who struggle with stress-related difficulties, executive functioning deficits, and ADHD in school settings and in private practice.

James W. Forgan, Ph.D., is an associate professor and Licensed School Psychologist. He teaches others how to teach and assess children with ADHD, executive functioning difficulty, and other types of learning disabilities at Florida Atlantic University. In private practice, he works with families of children with ADHD, EF, and other learning differences. Jim consults with public and private schools doing workshops on ADHD, executive functioning, dyslexia, problem solving, and accommodations for learning disabilities. You may reach him at http://jimforgan.com.

Mary Anne Richey, M.Ed., is a Licensed School Psychologist in a private practice providing evaluation of children with learning differences, consultations in private and public schools, and workshops on ADHD, executive functioning difficulties, and gifted students. She also has experience as a middle school teacher, administrator, high school guidance counselor, and adjunct college instructor. In 2012, she was honored as School Psychologist of the Year by the Florida Association of School Psychologists and was a nominee for the 2013 National School Psychologist of the Year, chosen by the National Association of School Psychologists.

Throughout this book, Jim and Mary Anne help parents manage the issues they face and incorporate strategies to help their children succeed in school and life. They have presented at national conventions and workshops for parents and professionals on strategies for helping those with ADHD and executive functioning difficulties maximize their potential. They are coauthors of *Raising Boys With ADHD*, *Raising Girls With ADHD*, *The Impulsive, Disorganized Child: Solutions for Parenting Kids With Executive Functioning Difficulties*, and *Stressed Out!: Solutions to Help Your Child Manage and Overcome Stress*. They share an integrated perspective on ADHD and executive functioning based on their experiences as parents and professionals, their academic research, and their interactions with so many other parents raising girls and boys with executive functioning difficulty and ADHD.